ARTFUL ARCHES

by Knit Picks

Photography by Amy Cave

Printed in the United States of America

Third Printing, 2019

ISBN 978-1-62767-158-3

Versa Press, Inc
800-447-7829

www.versapress.com

CONTENTS

Basketwork Socks   6

Rainbow Wave Socks   10

Oblique Socks   14

Tree of Life Socks   18

Meandering Socks   24

Mock Turtle Socks   28

Geometric Diamonds Socks   34

Twirla Socks   40

Westney Socks   44

Oscillatory Socks   48

Heavenly Shades Socks   52

Sparkle Socks   58

BASKETWORK SOCKS

by Mone Dräger

FINISHED MEASUREMENTS

7.5 (8, 8.75)" leg circumference, 8 (8.5, 9)" leg length including heel, foot length 8 (9, 10)"

YARN

Knit Picks Stroll Hand Painted Sock Yarn (75% Superwash Merino Wool, 25% Nylon; 462 yards/100g): Coffee Shop 25899, 1 skein

NEEDLES

US 1 ½ (2.5mm) two 24" circular needles for two circulars technique, or one 32" or longer circular needle for Magic Loop technique, or size to obtain gauge. (DPN's are not recommended due to construction)

NOTIONS

Yarn Needle
Stitch Markers

GAUGE

32 sts and 44 rows = 4" over Basketwork Pattern, blocked

Basketwork Socks

Notes:

The socks are knit toe-up with gusset and heel flap. The foot length and leg length are adjustable. Start gusset and cuff after the desired number of repeats of the pattern, but after having worked the pattern round indicated in the instructions. Foot should measure 4 (4, 4.25)" less than the desired length when starting the gusset.

Slip all stitches purlwise with yarn in back unless otherwise instructed in the pattern. Because of the slipped stitches and the crosses they form, the stitch pattern has less give than other patterns. Make sure to keep your tension even to meet gauge. If possible try on the sock frequently, especially when working the leg and if necessary adjust the leg length to make sure the sock is stretchy enough to be pulled on comfortably.

Double Wrap (DW)

To avoid the negative ease caused by the slipped stitches used in the cables, they are worked with double wraps. When the stitch is knit the yarn is wrapped twice around the needle; the additional wrap is dropped when working the stitch the next time.

1/2 LC

On RS: Slip next stitch to cable needle and place at front of work, K2, then K1 from cable needle.
On WS: Slip next 2 stitches to cable needle and place at back of work, P1, then P2 from cable needle.

1/2 LC DW

On RS: Slip next stitch to cable needle and place at front of work, K1 with a double wrap, K1, then K1 from cable needle.
On WS: Slip next 2 stitches to cable needle and place at back of work, P1, then P1, P1 with a double wrap from cable needle.

1/2 RC

Slip next 2 stitches to cable needle and place at back of work, K1, then K2 from cable needle.

1/2 RC DW

Slip next 2 stitches to cable needle and place at back of work, K1, then K1, K1 with a double wrap from cable needle.

Make 1 Left (M1L)

Lift the horizontal thread between your needles with your left needle tip from front to back. Knit this newly lifted stitch through the back loop.

Make 1 Left with Double Wrap (M1L DW)

Lift the horizontal thread between your needles with your left needle tip from front to back. Knit this newly lifted stitch through the back loop with a double wrap.

Make 1 Right (M1R)

Lift the horizontal thread between your needles with your left needle tip from back to front. Knit this newly lifted stitch.

Make 1 Right with Double Wrap (M1R DW)

Lift the horizontal thread between your needles with your left needle tip from back to front. Knit this newly lifted stitch with a double wrap.

Wrap and Turn (W&T)

Bring the yarn to the front, slip the next stitch purlwise, bring the yarn to the back, return the slipped stitch to its original position on the left needle. Turn your work.

Judy's Magic Cast On

Step 1: With your right hand, hold the needles together with the tips pointing left. Leaving a tail which is long enough to cast on the required number of stitches plus a little excess and place it between the top needle and the bottom needle and coming out to the back. Now, loop the working yarn over the top needle.
Step 2: Pick up the yarns with your left hand, holding the yarn tail over your index finger and the working yarn over your thumb in the slingshot position. This puts a little twist in the yarn which forms the first stitch on the top needle which is considered the first stitch.
Step 3: Move the pair of needles up and wrap the yarn on your index finger around the bottom needle as if making a yarn over.
Step 4: Move the needles downward and wrap the yarn on your thumb around the top needle as if making a yarn over.
Repeat steps 3 and 4 until you have the required number of stitches on both needles, ending with step 3.
Step 5: Turn the needles and take them in your left hand, so that the yarn tails are positioned at the right. Drop the tail and bring the working yarn up behind the top needle, making sure the tail lies under the working yarn to secure it. Knit the stitches of the top needle. Once these are worked, turn needles and knit the stitches on the second needle. 1 round worked.

Jeny's Surprisingly Stretchy Bind-off

Processing a K st: Wrap the yarn around the right-hand needle in a reverse yarn over, from back to front. K 1 st. Pull the YO over the K st.
Processing a P st: Warp the yarn around the right-hand needle in a yarn over, from front to back. P 1 st. Pull the YO over the P st.
BO Step 1: Work first st as described above; 1 st on the RH needle.
BO Step 2: Process the next st correctly, i.e. working the YO the way described above and K or P as needed.
BO Step 3: Pull the 1st st on your RH needle over the 2nd st on your RH needle and off the needle.
Repeat Steps 2 and 3 until 1 st remains. Cut the yarn and pull it through the last st.

Basketwork Instep Pattern (worked in the round over a multiple of 3 sts plus 2 sts)

Rnd 1: K2, *Sl1 WYIB, K2; rep from * to end.
Rnd 2: Rep Rnd 1.
Rnd 3: *1/2 RC DW; rep from * to last 2 sts, K2.
Rnds 4-5: Rep Rnds 1 and2.
Rnd 6: K2, *1/2 LC DW; rep from * to end.

Basketwork Heel Flap Pattern (worked in rows over a multiple of 3 sts plus 2 sts)

Row 1 (WS): P2, *Sl1 WYIF, P2; rep from * to end.
Row 2 (RS): K2, *Sl1 WYIB, K2; rep from * to end.
Row 3: *1/2 LC DW; rep from * to last 2 sts, P2.
Row 4: Rep Row 2.
Row 5: Rep Row 1.
Row 6: K2, *1/2 RC DW; rep from * to end.

Basketwork Leg Pattern (worked in rounds over a multiple of 3 sts)

Due to the nature of the pattern, there are cables worked using stitches at the end of one round and the beginning of the next round. The beginning of the round however stays in the same place. Pay careful attention to keep the marker at the correct position.

Rnd 1: *K2, Sl1; rep from * to end.
Rnd 2: K2, *1/2 LC DW; rep from * to last st, Sl1 to CN, remove M, K1 with DW, PM for beginning of rnd.
Rnd 3: K1, K1 from CN, *Sl1, K2; rep from to last st, Sl1.
Rnd 4: Rep Rnd 1.
Rnd 5: *1/2 RC DW; rep from * to end.
Rnd 6: Rep Rnd 1.

DIRECTIONS

Toe

Use Judy's Magic Cast On to cast on 20 (22, 24) sts; 10 (11, 12) sts on each needle. PM to indicate the beginning of the round.
Knit one round.
Inc Rnd: On Needle 1, *K1, M1L, K to last st, M1R, K1; rep from * on Needle 2. 24 (26, 28) sts.
Rep Inc Rnd four more times. 40 (42, 44) sts.
Next round: K
Alternate between Inc Rnd and plain K rnds until there are 60 (66, 72) sts; 30 (33, 36) sts on each needle.

Foot

Set-Up Rnd 1: Remove M, K all sts on Needle 1, K1 st from Needle 2 onto Needle 1, K all but the last stitch on Needle 2, transfer last st to Needle 1. 32 (35, 38) sts on Needle 1 for instep, 28 (31, 34) sts on Needle 2 for sole.
Set-Up Rnd 2: K2, [K1 with DW, K2] 10 (11, 12) times, K all sts of Needle 2.
Rnd 1: Work in Basketwork Instep pattern on Needle 1, K all sts on Needle 2.

Repeat Rnd 1, working Rnds 1-6 of Basketwork Instep pattern a total of four (five, six) times, then work Rnds 1-5 once more.

Gusset

Rnd 1: K2, *1/2 LC DW; rep from * to end of Needle 1, M1R DW, K sts of Needle 2. 1 st inc.
Rnd 2: *K2, Sl1; rep from * to end of Needle 1, K sts of Needle 2.
Rnd 3: *K2, Sl1; rep from * to end of Needle 1, M1R, K sts of Needle 2. 1 st inc.
Rnd 4: M1L DW, *1/2 RC DW; rep from * to last st of Needle 1, K1, K sts of Needle 2. 1 st inc.
Rnd 5: *Sl1, K2; rep from * to last 2 sts of Needle 1, Sl1, K1, M1R, K sts of Needle 2. 1 st inc.
Rnd 6: M1L, *Sl1, K2; rep from * to end of Needle 1, K sts of Needle 2. 1 st inc.
Rnd 7: K1, *1/2 LC DW; rep from * to end of Needle 1, M1R DW, K sts of Needle 2. 1 st inc.
Rnd 8: M1L, K1, *Sl1, K2; rep from * to last sts of Needle 1, Sl1, K sts of Needle 2. 1 st inc.
Rep Rnds 3-8 four more times. 91 (97, 103) sts; 63 (66, 69) on Needle 1 for instep, 28 (31, 34) on Needle 2 for sole.
Rnd 33: *K2, Sl1; rep from * to end of Needle 1, Sl1, K sts of Needle 2.

Set-Up for Short Row Heel: M1L, [1/2 RC] 5 times, [1/2 RC DW] 10 (11, 12) times, [1/2 RC] 6 times, do not work sole sts on Needle 2. 92 (98, 104) sts.

Heel Shaping (on Needle 2)

Row 1 (RS): K25 (28, 31), W&T.
Row 2 (WS): P22 (25, 28), W&T.
Row 3: K to 2 sts before st wrapped in previous RS row, W&T.
Row 4: P to 2 sts before st wrapped in previous WS row, W&T.

Rep Rows 3-4 three (three, four) more times.

Next Row (RS): K to end of needle. For all wrapped sts, pick up the wrap with the right needle from front to back, K the wrapped st and pull the yarn through both, the wrapped st and the wrap.
Next Row (WS): Sl1, P to end of needle. For all wrapped sts, pick up the wrap with the right needle from back to front, place it on the left needle and bring it over and behind the st it was wrapping, P the st together with the wrap.

Heel Flap

The heel flap is joined with the gusset sts at the end of each row. You might want to rearrange sts before you start working the heel flap and transfer first 16 sts and last 16 sts of Needle 1 to Needle 2. Adjust sts so that the first st to work is the last st worked for the heel.
Set-up Row (RS): Sl1, [K2, K1 with DW] 8 (9, 10) times, K2, SSK, turn. 1 gusset st dec.
Row 1 (WS): *Sl1 WYIF, P2; rep from * to last heel st, P2tog, turn. 1 gusset st dec.
Row 2 (RS): *Sl1, K2; rep from * to last st before gap, SSK, turn. 1 gusset st dec.
Row 3: Sl1 WYIF, *1/2 LC DW; rep from * to last 3 sts before gap, P2, P2tog, turn. 1 gusset st dec.
Row 4: Rep Row 2.
Row 5: Rep Row 1.
Row 6: Sl1, *1/2 RC DW; rep from * to last 3 sts before gap, K2, SSK, turn. 1 gusset st dec.
Rep Rows 1-6 three more times, then work Rows 1-5 once more. 62, (68, 74) sts.
Row 30: Sl1, *1/2 RC DW; rep from * to 3 sts before gap, Sl2 to CN and hold at back, K1, K1 from CN, SSK with DW (1 from CN and last gusset st), PM for beginning of rnd. 1 st dec. 61 (67, 73) sts.

Leg

Set-Up Rnd: [K2, Sl1] 10 (11, 12) times, K2, K2tog with DW, [K2, Sl1] to end. 60 (66, 72) sts.
Work in Basketwork Leg pattern. Pay close attention that the beginning of rnd M stays in the correct place.
Work Rnds 1-6 a total of 7 (8, 9) times, then work Rnds 1-4 once more.
Next Rnd: *1/2 RC; rep from * to end.

Cuff

Rnd 1: *K2, P1; rep from * to end.
Rep Rnd 1 fifteen more times.
BO in pattern using Jeny's Surprisingly Stretchy Bind Off.

Finishing

Weave in ends, wash and block.

RAINBOW WAVE SOCKS

by Christina Danaee

FINISHED MEASUREMENTS

7.5" foot circumference, 7.75" leg circumference, 9" foot length, 6" leg length

YARN

Knit Picks Stroll Hand Painted Sock Yarn (75% Superwash Merino Wool, 25% Nylon; 462 yards/100g):MC Big Top 26735, 1 hank
Knit Picks Stroll Sock Yarn (75% Superwash Merino Wool, 25% Nylon; 231/50g):
C1 Wonderland Heather 25028, 1 ball

NEEDLES

US 1 (2.25mm) two 24" circular needles for two circulars technique, or one 32" or longer circular needle for Magic Loop technique, or size to obtain gauge
US 0 (2mm) two 24" circular needles for two circulars technique, or one 32" or longer circular needle for Magic Loop technique, or one size smaller than size used to obtain gauge.

B (2.25mm) Crochet Hook (optional, to assist with K4tog)

NOTIONS

Yarn Needle
Stitch Markers
Scrap yarn of similar weight and contrasting color

GAUGE

40 sts and 48 rnds = 4" over Wave Pattern in the round with larger needles, blocked.
34 sts and 48 rnds = 4" in St st in the round with larger needles, blocked.
Wave Pattern repeat 13 sts and 12 rows = 1.25" x 1" with larger needles.

Rainbow Wave Socks

Notes: This sock is worked from the toe-up using an afterthought heel. The top of the foot is knit in a lace pattern that is then worked in the round for the sock leg.

Wave Pattern (in the round over multiples of 13 sts)
Rnd 1: Using MC K4tog, (YO, K1) repeat 5 times, YO, K4tog
Rnd 2: Using C1 K.
Rnds 3 and 4: Using MC K.
Rnds 5-8: Repeat Rnds 1-4.
Rnd 9: Rep Rnd 1.
Rnd 10-12: Using MC K.
Repeat Rnds 1-12 for pattern.

Follow all chart rows from right to left, reading them as RS rows.

Judy's Magic Cast-On
Using circular needles Judy's Magic Cast-on creates a seamless toe for your socks. http://tutorials.knitpicks.com/wptutorials/judys-magic-cast-on/

Kitchener Stitch
The Kitchener stitch will join the live stitches of the heel together seamlessly. http://tutorials.knitpicks.com/wptutorials/go-your-own-way-socks-top-down-part-8-kitchener-stitch/

DIRECTIONS

Toe
Using MC and Judy's Magic Cast-On, cast-on 16 sts to larger needle. (8sts per needle)
Knit one round.

Increase rounds:
Rnd 1: *K1, MIR, K to last stitch on needle, MIL, K1. Rep from * for second needle. 4sts inc.
Rnd 2: K.
Rep Rnds 1 and 2 until there are 68sts (34 on each needle) ending after Rnd 2.

Set Up Rnd: K4, PM, K26, PM, K4, K across needle 2.

Foot
Rnd 1: K4, SM, work Wave Pattern twice, SM, K4. K across needle 2.
Rep Rnd 1 working through Rnds 1-12 of the Wave Pattern, changing colors as indicated, until the sock measures 7" or 2" less than desired foot length ending after Rnd 10 of the Wave Pattern.

Heel Setup Rnd:
Needle 1: (K1, M1R) 3 times, K1, SM, work Rnd 11 of Wave Pattern twice, SM, (K1, M1L) 3 times, K1.
Needle 2: (K1, M1R) 2 times, K to 3 sts before end of needle, (K1, M1L) 2 times, K1.
Needle 1 now has 40 sts, Needle 2 has 38 sts.

Heel
Needle 1: K to M, SM, work Rnd 12 of Wave Pattern twice, SM, K to end of needle.
Needle 2: Using a contrast color scrap yarn of similar weight, K38.

Return to right side of needle and K38 with working yarn. (You have now created a place to pick up stitches for your heel once the leg of your sock is completed.)

Leg
Needle 1: (K1, YO) 3 times, K4tog, SM, work Rnd 1 of Wave Pattern twice, SM, K4tog, (YO, K1) 3 times.
Needle 2: (YO, K1) twice, YO, K4tog, work Rnd 1 of Wave Pattern twice, PM, using C1 K6. This marker will indicate the new beginning of round; you may adjust stitches on your needles in a way that is more comfortable to work, or keep them as-is, making sure to work in pattern across gap between needles. Markers on Needle 1 are no longer needed and can be removed if desired. The 13st Wave Pattern is worked 6 times around leg.

Work leg in pattern until it measures 3" from afterthought heel, ending after Rnd 1 of Wave Pattern.

Cuff
Switch to smaller needle(s).

With C1
Rnd 1: K.
Rnds 2-3: P.
Switch to MC.
Rnd 4: K.
Rnds 5-8: Work Rnds 9-12 of Wave Pattern.
Rnd 9: Work Rnd 1 of Wave Pattern.
Switch to C1, breaking MC yarn and leaving a 3" tail.
Rnd 10: K.
Rnd 11: (P2, P2tog) repeat to last 2sts, P2. 59sts.
Rnd 12: P.

BO all sts loosely knit wise.

Afterthought Heel
Remove waste yarn and transfer each set of 38 live stitches onto 2 needles.

Starting with the bottom of the sock foot facing join MC and K across needle 1.

Continue around to K across needle 2.

Decreases:
Rnd 1: *K1, SSK, K to last 3 sts on needle, K2tog, K1. Repeat from * on needle 2.
Rnd 2: K.

Repeat Rnds 1 and 2 until 24 sts remain (12 sts on each needle). Break yarn, join live stitches together using Kitchener stitch.

Finishing
Soak and block socks to desired measurements. Weave in ends.

Wave Pattern Chart

	13	12	11	10	9	8	7	6	5	4	3	2	1	
														12
														11
														10
	/4\	O		O		O		O		O		O	/4\	9
														8
														7
														6
	/4\	O		O		O		O		O		O	/4\	5
														4
														3
														2
	/4\	O		O		O		O		O		O	/4\	1

Legend

k4tog
Knit four stitches together as one

yo
Yarn Over

knit
knit stitch

MC

C1

OBLIQUE SOCKS

by Mone Dräger

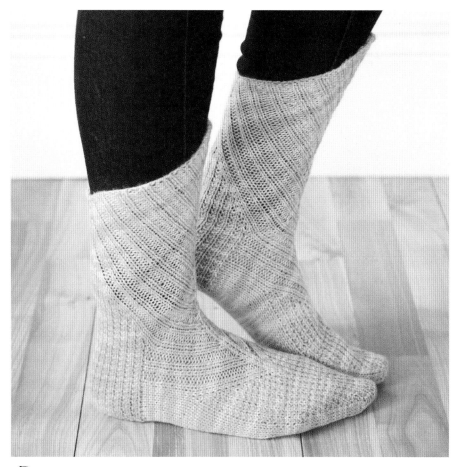

FINISHED MEASUREMENTS

Leg circumference 7 (8, 9)"; leg length at the back of the leg including heel 7 (7.75, 8.5)"; foot length 7 (8.25, 9.25)", adjustable

YARN

Knit Picks Hawthorne Kettle Dye (80% Superwash Fine Highland Wool, 20% Polyamide; 357 yards/100g): Compass 26690, 1 (1, 2) skein(s)

NEEDLES

US 2 (2.75mm) DPNs or two 24" circular needles for two circulars technique, or one 32" or longer circular needle for Magic Loop technique, or size to obtain gauge

NOTIONS

Yarn Needle
Stitch Markers

GAUGE

30 sts and 40 rows = 4" in St st in the rnd, blocked

Oblique Socks

Notes:

These top down socks with a heel flap and gusset feature ribbing patterns all over, while increases and decreases form the oblique lines. The ribbing patterns give a snug yet comfortable fit. Because of the way the increases and decreases are worked, the cuff is skewed so the socks are taller at the front.

Make 1 Left-Leaning Knit St (M1L): Lift the horizontal thread between your needles with your left needle tip from front to back. K the newly picked up st TBL. 1 st inc.

Make 1 Right-Leaning Knit St (M1R): Lift the horizontal thread between your needles with your left needle tip from back to front; K the newly picked up st. 1 st inc.

Make 1 Left-Leaning Purl St (M1LP): Lift the horizontal thread between your needles with your left needle tip from front to back. P the newly picked up stitch TBL. 1 st inc.

Make 1 Right-Leaning Purl St (M1RP): Lift the horizontal thread between your needles with your left needle tip from back to front, P the newly picked up st. 1 st inc.

2x2 Rib (worked over a multiple of 4 sts)
Rnd 1: *K2, P2; rep from * to end.
Rep Rnd 1 for pattern.
Please note: Due to the increases and decreases made in the ribbing section, the pattern might start in the middle of the repeat and also end a st early. When the pattern refers to 'work in 2x2 Rib' always work the sts as they appear, i.e. knit the knit sts, purl the purl sts.

Mistake Rib Pattern (worked in the rnd over a multiple of 2 sts plus 1 st)
Rnd 1: K.
Rnd 2: *K1, P1; rep from * to last st, K1.
Rep Rnds 1-2 for pattern.

Kitchener Stitch (grafting)
With an equal number of sts on two needles, thread end of working yarn through yarn needle. Hold needles parallel with RS facing and both needles pointing to the right. Perform Step 2 on the first front st, and then Step 4 on the first back st, and then continue with instructions below.
Step 1: Pull yarn needle K-wise though front st and drop st from knitting needle.
Step 2: Pull yarn needle P-wise through next front st, leave st on knitting needle.
Step 3: Pull yarn needle P-wise through first back st and drop st from knitting needle.
Step 4: Pull yarn needle K-wise through next back st, leave st on knitting needle.
Rep Steps 1 – 4 until all sts have been grafted.

DIRECTIONS

Leg Section 1
Loosely CO 58 (66, 74) sts. Join to work in the rnd and PM, being careful not to twist sts.

Rnd 1: K2, (P2, K2) 6 (7, 8) times, P2, K1, PM, K1, (P2, K2) 7 (8, 9) times.
Rnd 2: (K2, P2) to last 2 sts, K2.
Rnd 3: K2, M1L, (P2, K2) to 3 sts before M, P1, K2tog, SM, SSK, P1, (K2, P2) to last 2 sts, M1R, K2.
Rnd 4: K3, (P2, K2) to 2 sts before M, P1, K1, SM, K1, P1, (K2, P2) to last 3 sts, K3.
Rnd 5: K2, M1L, K1, (P2, K2) to 2 sts before M, K2tog, SM, SSK, (K2, P2) to last 3 sts, K1, M1R, K2.
Rnd 6: K4, (P2, K2) to 1 st before M, K1, SM, K3, (P2, K2) to last 2 sts, K2.
Rnd 7: K2, M1LP, (K2, P2) to 3 sts before M, K1, K2tog, SM, SSK, K1, (P2, K2) to last 2 sts, M1RP, K2.
Rnd 8: K2, P1, (K2, P2) to 2 sts before M, K2, SM, (K2, P2) to last 5 sts, K2, P1, K2.
Rnd 9: K2, M1LP, P1, (K2, P2) to 2 sts before M, K2tog, SM, SSK, (P2, K2) to last 3 sts, P1, M1RP, K2.
Rnd 10: (K2, P2) to 1 st before M, K1, SM, K1, (P2, K2) to end.

Rep Rnds 3-10 one more time.

Leg Section 2
Rnd 1: M1L, K2, (P2, K2) to 3 sts before M, P1, K2tog, SM, SSK, P1, (K2, P2) to last 2 sts, K2. 57 (65, 73) sts.
Rnd 2: P1, PM (K2, P2) to 4 sts before M, K2, P1, K1, SM, K1, P1, (K2, P2) to last 2 sts, K2.
Rnd 3: M1L, K to M, M1R, SM, (K2, P2) to 4 sts before M, K2, K2tog, SM, SSK, (K2, P2) to last 2 sts, K2.
Rnd 4: (K1, P1) to 1 st before M, K1, SM, (K2, P2) to 3 sts before M, K3, SM, K3, (P2, K2) to end.
Rnd 5: M1L, K to M, M1R, SM, (K2, P2) to 3 sts before M, K1, K2tog, SM, SSK, K1, (P2, K2) to end.
Rnd 6: (P1, K1) to 1 st before M, P1, SM, (K2, P2) to 2 sts before M, K2, SM, (K2, P2) to last 2 sts, K2.
Rnd 7: M1L, K to M, M1R, SM, (K2, P2) to 2 sts before M, K2tog, SM, SSK, (P2, K2) to end.
Rnd 8: (K1, P1) to 1 st before M, K1, SM, (K2, P2) to 1 st before M, K1, SM, K1, (P2, K2) to end.
Rnd 9: M1L, K to M, M1R, SM, (K2, P2) to 5 sts before M, K2, P1, K2tog, SM, SSK, P1, (K2, P2) to last 2 sts, K2.
Rnd 10: (P1, K1) to 1 st before M, P1, SM, (K2, P2) to 4 sts before M, K2, P1, K1, SM, K1, P1, (K2, P2) to last 2 sts, K2.

Rep Rnds 3-10 2 (3, 3) more times. 25 (33, 33) sts in Mistake Rib before first M.

Size 7" and 9" Only: Rep Rnds 3-6 once more. 29 (33, 37) sts in Mistake Rib before first M.

Heel Flap
The heel flap is worked back and forth in rows over the first 29 (33, 37) sts of the rnd. Keep remaining 28 (32, 36) sts on hold for instep.

Row 1 (RS): Sl1 WYIB, K28 (32, 36).
Row 2 (WS): Sl1 WYIF, (P1, K1) to last 2 sts, P2.
Rep Rows 1-2 12 (13, 14) more times.

Turn Heel
Short-Row 1 (RS): Sl1 WYIB, K15 (17, 19), SSK, K1, turn.
Short-Row 2 (WS): Sl1 WYIF, P4, P2tog, P1, turn.

Short-Row 3: Sl1 WYIB, K to 1 sts before gap, SSK, K1, turn.
Short-Row 4: Sl1 WYIF, P to 1 sts before gap, P2tog, P1, turn.
Rep Short-Rows 3-4 4 (5, 6) more times. 17 (19, 21) heel sts.

Gusset

Set-up Rnd 1: Sl1 WYIB, K16 (18, 20), PU and K13 (14, 15) sts along the edge of the heel flap, work instep sts as established in 2x2 Rib to 2 sts before M, K2tog, SM, SSK, work sts as established in 2x2 Rib to end of instep, PU and K13 (14, 15) sts along the edge of the heel flap, K22 (25, 28), PM for new beginning of rnd. 69 (77, 85) sts.
Set-up Rnd 2: (K2, P2) twice, work sts as established in 2x2 Rib to 1 st before M, K1, SM, K1, work sts as established in 2x2 Rib to end of instep, (P2, K2) twice, PM, K to end.
Dec Rnd: Work in 2x2 Rib to 2 sts before M, K2tog, SM, SSK, work in 2x2 Rib to next M, K to end. 2 sts dec.
Next Rnd: Work in 2x2 Rib to 1 sts before M, K1, SM, K1, work in 2x2 Rib to next M, K to end.

Rep last two rnds 6 more times. 55 (63, 71) sts.

Foot Section 1

Rnd 1: M1R, PM, work in 2x2 Rib to 2 sts before M, K2tog, SM, SSK, work in 2x2 Rib to next M, SM, M1L, PM, K to end.
Rnd 2: P1, SM, work in 2x2 Rib to 1 st before M, K1, SM, K1, work in 2x2 Rib to next M, SM, P1, SM, K to end.
Rnd 3: K to M, M1R, SM, work in 2x2 Rib to 2 sts before M, K2tog, SM, SSK, work in 2x2 Rib to next M, SM, M1L, K to M, SM, K to end.
Rnd 4: (P1, K1) to M, SM, work in 2x2 Rib to 1 st before M, K1, SM, K1, work in 2x2 Rib to next M, SM, (K1, P1) to M, SM, K to end.
Rnd 5: Rep Rnd 3.
Rnd 6: (P1, K1) to 1 st before M, P1, SM, work in 2x2 Rib to 1 st before M, K1, SM, K1, work in 2x2 Rib to next M, SM, (P1, K1) to 1 st before M, P1, SM, K to end.

Rep Rnds 3-6 (ending on a Rnd 4 or Rnd 6) until there is only 1 st left each between first and second, and second and third marker, i.e. the markers in the middle of the instep. Remove second and third marker on last rnd.

Next Rnd: K to M, remove M, K2tog, K to end. 54 (62, 70) sts; 27 (31, 35) sts each on instep and sole.
Foot length measures approximately 5 (6, 6.5)" at this point.

Foot Section 2

Rnd 1: (P1, K1) to 1 st before M, P1, SM, K to end.
Rnd 2: Knit.
Rep Rows 1-2 until foot measures 1.75 (2, 2.5)" less than desired foot length.

Rep Rnd 1 once more.

Toe

Rnd 1: *K1, SSK, K to 3 sts before M, K2tog, K1; rep from * once. 4 sts dec.
Rnd 2: K3, (P1, K1) to 2 sts before M, K2, SM, K to end.
Rnd 3: Rep Rnd 1.
Rnd 4: K2, (P1, K1) to 1 sts before M, K1, SM, K to end
Rep Rnds 1-4 3 (4, 5) more times. 22 sts.
Rep Rnd 1 once more. 18 sts.

Cut yarn, leaving an 18" tail. Use the yarn needle and tail and graft the instep sts to the sole sts, using Kitchener Stitch.

Finishing

Weave in ends, wash and block lightly.

TREE OF LIFE SOCKS

by Kate Lonsdale

FINISHED MEASUREMENTS

7 (8, 9)" leg circumference; 9 (10, 11)" foot length, unstretched

YARN

Knit Picks Stroll Hand Painted Sock Yarn (75% Superwash Merino Wool, 25% Nylon; 462 yards/100 g): MC Koi Pond 26736, 1 hank.

Knit Picks Stroll Sock Yarn (75% Superwash Merino Wool, 25% Nylon; 231 yards/50 g): C1 Black 23701, 1 ball

NEEDLES

US 1.5 (2.5mm) DPNs or two 24" circular needles for two circulars technique, or one 32" or longer circular needle for Magic Loop technique, or size to obtain gauge

NOTIONS

Yarn Needle

GAUGE

32 sts and 48 rnds = 4" in St st in the round, blocked

Tree Of Life Socks

Notes:

This sock pattern was inspired by Frank Lloyd Wright's famous "Tree of Life" windows in the Darwin D. Martin house. While the pattern looks intricate, all colorwork is worked using slip stitches which means that you are only working with one color at a time. Be careful to catch the non-working yarn at the beginning of each round to carry it along. Instructions for the Leg and Foot sections are charted as well as written out. Each row on the charts is a RS round and should be read from right to left.

YOB - yarn over backwards

At the beginning of a WS row, move the working yarn to the back as if to knit, insert right-hand needle into first st purlwise, bring working yarn over right-hand needle and complete the first purl st as usual, creating an extra st before the first purl. (Note: This extra st will be mounted backwards. When you work this st later, you will need to reorient it in the correct position before you knit it.)

K3tog - K 3 together

Knit three stitches together as one.

SSSP

Sl the next 3 sts as if to K, move these 3 sts back to the left-hand needle, P these 3 sts together through the back loop

DIRECTIONS

Cuff

CO 56 (64, 72) sts in C1 and join for working in the round. Be careful not to twist your sts.

Rnd 1: *P1, K3, rep from * until end of rnd.

Change to MC and rep Rnd 1 until cuff measures 2 (2, 2.5)" from CO edge.

Knit 3 rounds in St st.

Leg

Beginning of Chart A
Rnd 1 (C1): *Sl1, K3, rep from * until end of rnd.
Rnd 2 (MC): K.
Rnd 3 (C1): *Sl1, K1, rep from * until end of rnd.
Rnd 4 (MC): K.
Rnd 5 (C1): *Sl1, K3, rep from * until end of rnd.
Rnd 6 (MC): K.
Rnd 7 (C1): *Sl1, K3, rep from * until end of rnd.
Rnd 8 (MC): K.
Rnd 9 (C1): *Sl1, K1, rep from * until end of rnd.
Rnd 10 (MC): K.
Rnd 11 (C1): *Sl1, K3, rep from * until end of rnd.
Rnd 12 (MC): *K2, Sl1, K1, rep from * until end of rnd.

Repeat Rnds 11& 12, 5 (7, 9) more times.

Rnd 23 (27,31) (C1): *Sl1, K3, rep from * until end of rnd.
End of Chart A

Rnds 1-3 (MC): K.
Rnd 4 (C1): K.

Rnd 5 (MC): K.
Rnd 6 (C1): K.
Rnds 7-9 (MC): K.
Rnd 10 (C1): K.

Heel

Heel is worked back and forth with short rows in C1. Do not break MC, it will be picked up in the next section.

You may substitute another method or an afterthought heel if you prefer, however the heel flap method is not recommended, as it does not reflect the symmetry of the Prairie style.

Right Heel is worked on the first 28 (32, 36) sts, and the remaining 28 (32, 36) sts are K in C1 after the heel is complete. For the Left Heel, K the first 28 (32, 36) sts in C1, then complete the heel on the remaining 28 (32, 36) sts.

Row 1 Right Sock (RS): K27 (31, 35), turn.
Row 1 Left Sock (RS): K55 (63, 71), turn.
(Left and Right Socks are worked the same way from here until the last rnd.)
Row 2 (WS): YOB, P26 (30, 34), turn
Row 3: YO, K25 (29, 33), turn
Row 4: YOB, P24 (28, 32), turn
Rows 5-22: Repeat Rows 3-4 9 more times, working 1 fewer st in each row- 6 (10, 14) sts remain between YOs.
Row 23: YO, K6 (10, 14), remount the next st (the YOB from previous row) and K2tog with the following st, turn.
Row 24: YOB, P7 (11, 15), SSP, turn.
Row 25: YO, K8 (12, 16), remount next 2 sts, K3tog (with the 2 remounted sts and the next st), turn.
Row 26: YOB, P9 (13, 17), SSSP, turn.
Rows 27-42: Repeat Rows 25-26, eight more times, working one more st in each row. 25 (29, 33) purled sts in the center section.
Row 43: YO, K26 (30, 34), remount next 2 sts, K3tog (with the 2 remounted sts and the next st), turn.
Row 44: P27 (31, 35), SSP, turn. No unworked sts remain.

For Right Sock only: With C1, K 1 rnd.
For Left Sock only: With C1, K28 (32, 36).

For both socks, you should be back at the beginning of the rnd. 56 (64, 72) sts.

Foot

Rnd 1 (C1): K.
Rnds 2-4 (MC): K.
Rnd 5 (C1): K.
Rnd 6 (MC): K.
Rnd 7 (C1): K.
Rnds 8-10 (MC): K.

Beginning of Chart B
Rnd 1 (C1): *Sl1, K3, rep from * until end of rnd.
Rnd 2 (MC): K.
Rnd 3 (C1): *Sl1, K1, rep from * until end of rnd.
Rnd 4 (MC): K.
Rnd 5 (C1): *Sl1, K3, rep from * until end of rnd.
Rnd 6 (MC): K.
Rnd 7 (C1): *Sl1, K3, rep from * until end of rnd.

Rnd 8 (MC): *K2, Sl1, K1, rep from * until end of rnd.

Rnds 9-18 (9-22, 9-26): Rep rnds 7 & 8, 5 (7, 9) more times.

Rnd 19 (23, 27) (C1): *Sl1, K3, rep from * until end of rnd.

Rnd 20 (24, 28) (MC): K.

Rnd 21 (25, 29) (C1): *K3, Sl1, rep from * until end of rnd.

Rnd 22 (26, 30) (MC): K.

Rnd 23 (27, 31) (C1): *K1, Sl1, rep from * until end of rnd.

Rnd 24 (28, 32) (MC): *Sl1, K1, rep from * until end of rnd.

Rnds 25-28 (29-32, 33-36): Rep rnds 23 & 24 (27 & 28, 31 & 32), two more times.

Rnd 29 (33, 37) (C1): *K1, Sl1, rep from * until end of rnd.

Rnd 30 (34, 38) (MC): K.

Rnd 31 (35, 39) (C1): *K3, Sl1, rep from * until end of rnd.

Rnd 32 (36, 40) (MC): K.

Rnd 33 (37, 41) (C1): *Sl1, K3, rep from * until end of rnd.

Rnd 34 (38, 42) (MC): *K2, Sl1, K1, rep from * until end of rnd.

Rnd 35 (39, 43) (C1): *Sl1, K3, rep from * until end of rnd.

Rnds 36-45 (40-53, 44-61): rep rnds 34 & 35 (38 & 39, 42 & 43), 5 (7, 9) times.

Rnd 46 (54, 62) (MC): K.

Rnd 47 (55, 63) (C1): *Sl1, K3, rep from * until end of rnd.

Rnd 48 (56, 64) (MC): K.

Rnd 49 (57, 65) (C1): *Sl1, K1, rep from * until end of rnd.

Rnd 50 (58, 66) (MC): K.

Rnd 51 (59, 67) (C1): *Sl1, K3, rep from * until end of rnd.

End of Chart B

Rnds 1-3 (MC): K.

Rnd 4 (C1): K.

Rnd 5 (MC): K.

Rnd 6 (C1): K.

Rnds 7-9 (MC): K.

Rnds 10-11 (CC): K.

Toe

Toe is worked in C1. Break MC and work in the yarn end on the inside of the sock in order to avoid having to weave it in later.

Rnd 1: K.

Rnd 2: *SSK, K24 (28, 32), K2tog, rep from * once. 52 (60, 68) sts.

Rnd 3: K.

Rnd 4: *SSK, K22 (26, 30), K2tog, rep from * once. 48 (56, 64) sts.

Rnd 5: K.

Cont in pattern as established, decreasing 4 sts every even-numbered rnd, until 14 sts remain on each needle – 14 (18, 22) rnds, 28 sts total.

Next Rnd: K.

Distribute half the sts onto each of two needles. Graft remaining sts together using Kitchener st.

Repeat instructions for second sock, remembering to work heel differently, as indicated, for Right and Left Socks.

Finishing

Weave in ends. Block to measurements.

Chart A

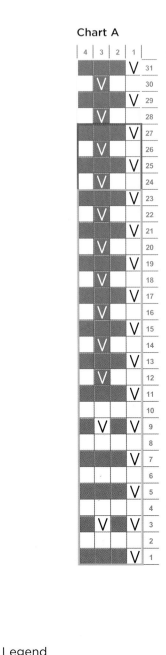

Chart B 9"

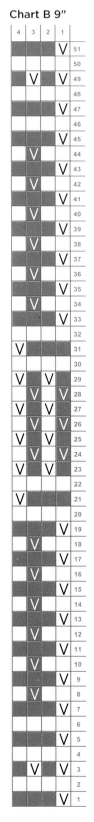

Chart B 10"

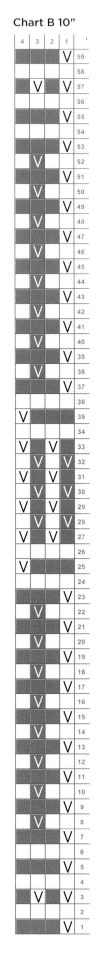

Chart B 11"

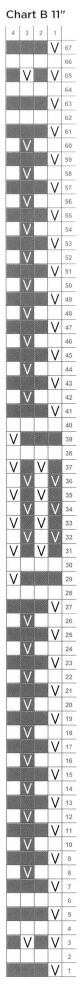

Legend

slip
|V| Slip stitch as if to purl, holding yarn in back

knit
knit stitch

9" finished length

10" finished length

11" finished length

MC

C1

MEANDERING SOCKS

by Dana Gervais

FINISHED MEASUREMENTS

7 (8, 9, 10)" finished circumference, choose a circumference that is 10% less than the wearer's actual foot circumference as measured at the widest part of the foot. Foot length is customizable

YARN

Knit Picks Stroll Hand Painted Sock Yarn (75% Superwash Merino Wool, 25% Nylon; 462 yards/100g): Gemstone 26738, 1 hank

NEEDLES

US 1 (2.25mm) DPNs, or two 24" circular needles for two circulars technique, or one 32" or longer circular needle for Magic Loop technique, or size to obtain gauge

NOTIONS

Yarn Needle
Stitch Markers
Cable Needle (optional)

GAUGE

32 sts and 48 rnds = 4" in St st in the round, blocked.
32 sts and 48 rnds = 4" in Meandering St pattern in the round, blocked

Meandering Socks

Notes:

These socks are worked top down beginning with a ribbed cuff. The Meandering stitch pattern starts at the top of the leg and continues on the top of the foot, while the back of the leg and sole of the foot are worked in stockinette. Featuring a short row heel and a wedge toe that is grafted closed with Kitchener Stitch, the pattern has written instructions provided for the smallest size with instructions for the other sizes appearing in parentheses. If there are no parentheses the instruction applies to all sizes.

A cable needle may be helpful (but not necessary) to hold the slipped stitch in front of work. All slipped sts are slipped purl wise.

Meandering Stitch Pattern (worked in the round over a multiple of 4 sts)

Rnd 1: *K3, K1 wrapping yarn twice around needle; rep from *.
Rnd 2: *P3, Sl1WYIB dropping the extra wrap; rep from *.
Rnd 3: *K3, Sl1WYIB; rep from *.
Rnd 4: *P3, Sl1WYIB; rep from *.
Rnd 5: *Sl3WYIB, Sl next st off LH needle to front of work, Sl same 3 sts back to LH needle, return Sl st to LH needle and K wrapping yarn twice around needle, K3; rep from *.
Rnd 6: *Sl1WYIB dropping the extra wrap, P3; rep from *.
Rnd 7: *Sl1WYIB, K3; rep from *.
Rnd 8: *Sl1WYIB, P3; rep from *.
Rnd 9: *Sl next st off LH needle to front of work, K3, return Sl st to LH needle and K wrapping yarn twice around needle; rep from *.

DIRECTIONS

Cuff

CO 56 (64, 72, 80) sts; PM after the 28th (32nd, 36th, 40th) st to divide sts as follows: the first 28 (32, 36, 40) sts will form the front of the leg/instep of the sock and the last 28 (32, 36, 40) sts will form the back of the leg/heel/sole of the sock. PM to mark beginning of rnd and join for working in the round being careful not to twist sts.

Rnd 1: (K1, P1) to end.
Repeat Rnd 1 twelve times or until work measures 1" from CO edge.

Leg

Set Up Rnd: Work Rnd 1 of Meandering St pattern until M, SM, K to end.

Work as established, working Meandering St pattern Rnds 1-9 once, then rep Rnds 2-9 of the Meandering St pattern until work measures 6" or desired length from CO edge.

Heel

The heel is worked back and forth across the last 28 (32, 36, 40) sts.

Set Up Rnd: Work the Meandering stitch pattern as established across the first 28 (32, 36, 40) sts. Note the last pattern rnd worked.

Row 1 (RS): Sl1, K26 (30, 34, 38), M1L, turn work.
Row 2 (WS): Sl1, P26, (30, 34, 38), M1P, turn work.
Row 3: Sl1, K25 (29, 33, 37), M1L, turn work.
Row 4: Sl1, P24 (28, 32, 36), M1P turn work.

Rep Rows 3 and 4, working one less st before the increase on each row until there are 8 (10, 12, 12) sts between increases, ending after a WS row.

Row 5 (RS): Sl1, K7 (9, 11, 11), SSK, K1, turn work.
Row 6 (WS): Sl1, P7 (9, 11, 11), P2tog, P1, turn work.
Row 7: Sl1, K8 (10, 12, 12), SSK, K1, turn work.
Row 8: Sl1, P9 (11, 13, 13), P2tog, P1, turn work.

Rep Rows 7 and 8, working one more st on each row before working the dec until all heel sts have been worked and 28 (32, 36, 40) heel sts remain ending after a WS row.

Foot

K across heel sts to beginning of rnd.

Cont working the Meandering St pattern as established across the first 28 (32, 36, 40) sts while working the last 28 (32, 36, 40) sts in St st until foot measures 1.75 (2, 2, 2.5)" less than desired finished length ending after any rnd except Rnds 5 or 9.

Toe

Rnd 1: *K1, SSK, K to 3 sts before M, K2tog, K1, SM; rep from * to end. 4 sts dec.
Rnd 2: K all sts.

Repeat Rnds 1-2 10 (12, 13, 15) times until 16 (16, 20, 20) sts remain.

Finishing

Arrange all instep sts on a single needle and all sole sts on a single needle. Use Kitchener Stitch to graft instep and sole sts together.

Weave in ends and block.

MOCK TURTLE SOCKS

by Mary E Rose

FINISHED MEASUREMENTS

6 (7, 8, 9)" foot circumference, and 6 (6.5, 7, 7.5)" leg length before heel. Foot length is adjustable

YARN

Knit Picks Stroll Hand Painted Sock Yarn (75% Superwash Merino Wool, 25% Nylon; 462 yards/100g): Northern Lights 26733, 1 hank

NEEDLES

US 1 (2.25mm) DPNs or two 24" circular needles for two circulars technique, or one 32" or longer circular needle for Magic Loop technique, or size to obtain gauge

NOTIONS

Yarn Needle
Stitch Markers

GAUGE

36 sts and 44 rnds = 4" over Mock Turtle stitch in the round, blocked.
32 sts and 44 rnds = 4" in St st in the round, blocked

Mock Turtle Socks

Notes:

With its 2x2 ribbing hugging the back of your leg, and a subdued textured patterning across the front and top of your foot, these socks allow hand painted, multi-colored or tonal yarns to shine and take center stage, while there's enough action in the slip stitch patterning to keep the knitter interested.

This top-down sock with a slipped stitch heel flap and standard gusset and toe comes in four sizes to fit children through adults.

When working the slipped stitches carry the yarn *very loosely* at the front of the work.

Follow all chart rows from right to left, reading them as RS rows.

DIRECTIONS

Cuff

CO 48 (56, 64, 72) stitches and join to begin working in the round, being careful not to twist sts.

Rnd 1: K1, *P2, K2* to last three sts, P2, K1.

Repeat Rnd 1 until cuff measures 1.5 (2, 2, 2)" from CO edge. If additional leg length is desired repeat Rnd 2 of the chart as needed.

Leg

Rnd 1: With the Leg Chart for your size, work Rnd 1 over first 24 (28, 32, 36) sts, K1, *P2, K2* to last 3 sts, P2, K1.. 49 (57, 65, 73) sts
Rnd 2: Work next Rnd of chart of first 25 (29, 33, 37) sts, K1, *P2, K2* to last 3 sts, P2, K1.

Repeat Rnd 2 until all Rnds of the chart have been worked.

6" Size Only

Rep chart Rnds 2-13 three more times for a total of 4 pattern repeats.

Proceed to heel flap.

Heel Flap

Heel is worked over the last 24 (28, 32, 36) sts of the round. After finishing final Chart Rnd turn work for Set Up Row.

Set Up Row (WS): Sl1, P23 (27, 31, 35).

Row 1 (RS): *Sl1, K1* rep from * to * to end. 24 (28, 32, 36) heel flap sts.
Row 2 (WS): Sl1, P23 (27, 31, 35).

Repeat Rows 1 and 2 a total of 12 (14, 16, 18) times.

Heel Turn

Row 1 (RS): Sl1 WYIB, K14 (16, 18, 20) SSK, K1, turn.
Row 2 (WS): Sl1 WYIF, P7, P2tog, P1, turn.
Row 3: Sl1 WYIB, K8, SSK, K1, turn.
Row 4: Sl1 WYIF, P9, P2tog, P1, turn.

Continue in this manner working one additional st before the decrease until all sts have been worked, ending with a WS row. 16 (18, 20, 22) heel flap sts.

Gusset

Set Up Rnd: Sl1, K to end of heel flap. PU & K13 (15, 17, 19) sts (1 for every slipped st) along edge of flap. Change needles or place instep marker here. Work Rnd 1 of Foot Chart for your size. Change needles, or place insole marker here. PU & K13 (15, 17, 19) sts along the second side of heel flap. K8 (9, 10, 11). Arrange needles or place marker here for start of round. 67 (77, 87, 97) sts.

Rnd 1: K to 3 sts before M, K2tog, K1, SM, work Leg Chart for appropriate size across instep sts, SM, K1, SSK, K to end of rnd. 2 sts dec.
Rnd 2: K to first marker, SM, work Leg Chart for appropriate size across instep sts, SM, K to end of rnd.

Repeat Rnds 1 and 2 until 49 (57, 65, 73) sts remain.

Foot

6" Size Only: Continue working chart rnds 2-13 on instep sts and St st for insole sts until foot measures 1.25" less than desired length, ending on Rnd 7 or 13. Decrease 1 st on instep sts on final rnd and proceed to Toe instructions. 48 sts.

All other sizes: Continue working Foot Chart on instep stitches and St st for insole stitches until chart for your size is complete. For a longer foot work additional rnds in St st until 1.5 (2, 2.25)" less than desired length. Proceed to Toe instructions. 56 (64, 72) sts.

Toe

Rnd 1: K to 3 sts before instep marker, K2tog, K1, SM, K1, SSK, K to 3 sts before insole marker, K2tog, K1, SM, K1, SSK, K to end of rnd. 4 sts dec.
Rnd 2: K.

Repeat Rnds 1 and 2 3 (5, 7, 9) more times. 32 sts.
Repeat Rnd 1 until 16 sts remain. K4 to side of sock.

Rearrange sts so that all the instep sts are on one needle and all the insole sts are on a second needle and graft the remaining sts together using Kitchener st.

Finishing

Weave in ends, wash and block on sock blockers.

Legend

	knit
□	**knit** knit stitch
–|V|–	**Slip 3 Sts** Slip 3 stitches purlwise holding yarn very loosely in front of work
◆	**Bow** Slip tip of working needle from the bottom to the top, under the strands from the slipped stitches, knit next stitch and pass strands over stitch just worked
⧄	**k2tog** Knit two stitches together as one stitch
■	**No Stitch** Placeholder - No stitch made.
M	**make one** Make one by lifting strand in between stitch just worked and the next stitch, knit into back of this thread.
□	pattern repeat

48 st foot and leg chart

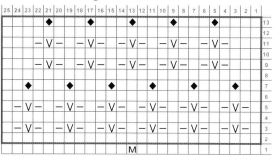

56 st Leg Chart

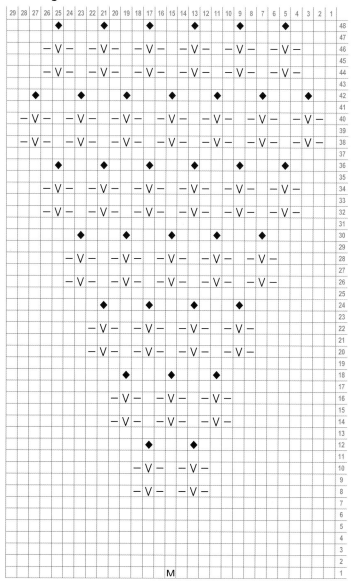

56 st Foot Chart

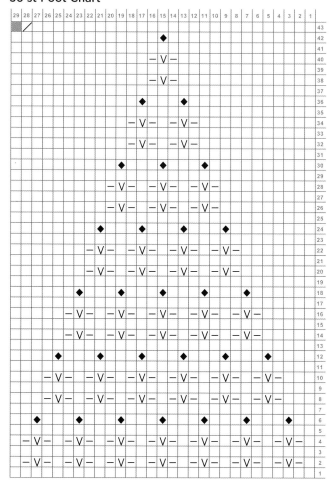

64 st Foot Chart

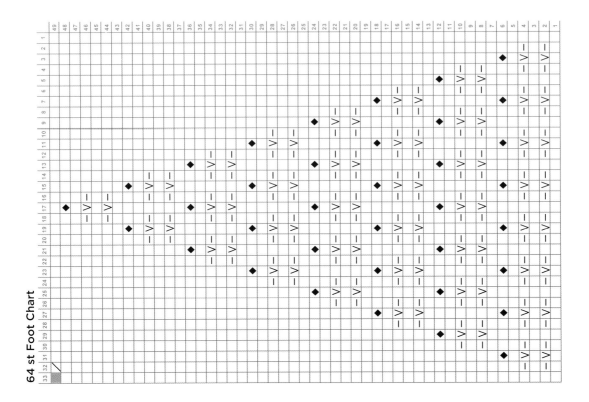

64 st Leg Chart

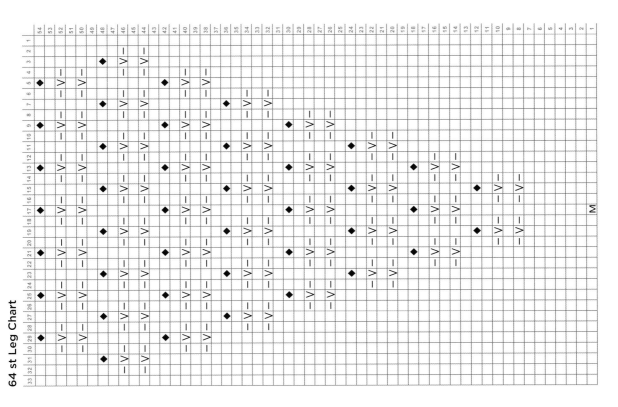

72 st Foot Chart

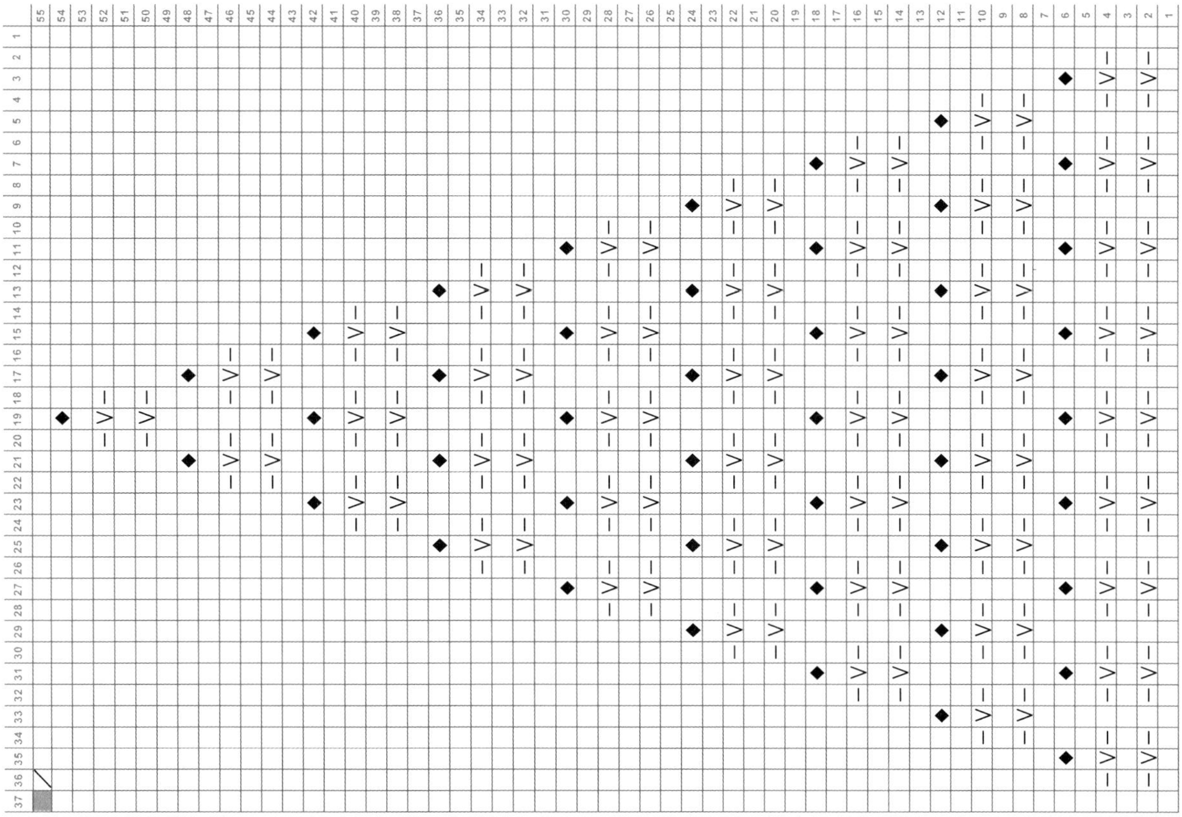

72 st Leg Chart

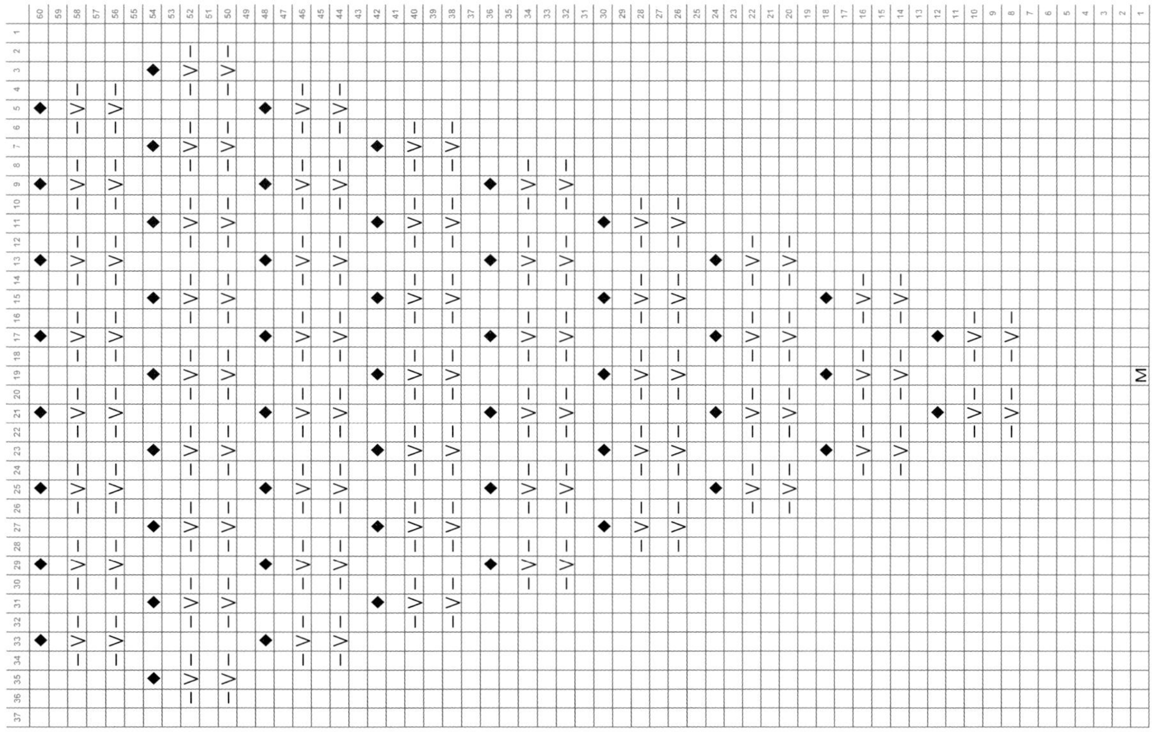

GEOMETRIC DIAMONDS SOCKS

by Becky Greene

FINISHED MEASUREMENTS

8 (9)" leg circumference (unstretched, blocked); foot length is adjustable

YARN

Knit Picks Stroll Hand Painted Sock Yarn (75% Superwash Merino Wool, 25% Nylon; 462 yards/100 g): MC Red Wing Blackbird 27073, 1 hank
Knit Picks Stroll Brights Sock Yarn (75% Superwash Merino Wool, 25% Nylon; 231 yards/50 g): C1 Electric Blue 26406, 1 ball

NEEDLES

US 2 (2.75mm) DPNs or two 24" circular needles for two circulars technique, or one 32" or longer circular needle for Magic Loop technique, or size to obtain gauge

NOTIONS

Yarn Needle
Stitch Markers
Scrap yarn or stitch holder

GAUGE

32 sts and 40 rnds = 4" in St st in the round, blocked.
32 sts and 37 rnds = 4" in Stranded St st in the round, blocked.

Geometric Diamonds Socks

Notes:

These eye-catching socks are knit from the cuff down in the round with a standard slip-stitch heel flap. Two options are given for working the color work charts: wide or narrow diamond lattice. The sample is made with the wide diamond charts.

For cleanest results, knit with the MC as the dominant color. A tutorial on Yarn Dominance can be found here: http://tutorials.knitpicks.com/fair-isle-knitting-tips-yarn-dominance/.

DIRECTIONS

Cuff

CO 64 (72) sts. PM. Join for working in the rnd, being careful not to twist sts.

Rnds 1-15: (K2,P2) to the end of the rnd.
Rnd 16: K.

Leg

Adding C1, begin to work from your choice of colorwork charts (Diamond chart or Skinny Diamond chart) for the correct size. Chart is worked twice per round. Work Rnds 1-16 (1-18) three times. Break off C1. Place last 32 (36) sts on holder for instep.

Heel

Row 1: (Sl1, K1) to end.
Row 2: Sl1, P to end.
Rep rows 1 & 2 14 times (or to desired heel depth).

Heel Turn

Row 1: Sl1, K18 (20), SSK, K1; turn.
Row 2: Sl1, P7, P2tog, P1; turn.
Row 3: Sl1, K to 1 st before gap, SSK, K1, turn.
Row 4: Sl1, P to 1 st before gap, P2tog, P1, turn.
Repeat rows 3 and 4 until all heel sts are worked. (20,22) sts.

Gusset

Rnd 1: K across heel sts; PU and K 1 st in each slipped st of the heel flap plus one extra in the corner before the instep; PM; K across instep; PM; PU and K 1 st in the corner between instep and side of heel, PU and K 1 st in each slipped st of the heel flap; K to first marker (beginning of instep is now the beginning of rnd).
Rnd 2: K to marker; SM: K1, SSK, K to last 3 sts before marker; K2tog, K1; SM. 2 sts dec.
Rnd 3: K, slipping M.

Rep Rnds 2 and 3 until there are 32 (36) sole sts again. 64 (72) sts total.

Foot

Continue to work in St st until foot measures 3" less than desired foot length. Work Diamond Foot chart or Skinny Diamond Foot chart for the correct size one time. Chart is worked twice per rnd. 8 (9) rnds worked.

K one rnd.

Toe

Rnd 1: (K1, SSK, K to 3 sts before marker, K2tog, K1, SM) twice. 4 sts dec.
Rnd 2: K.

Repeat Rnds 1 and 2 until there are 12 (16) sts remaining on each of instep and sole. Kitchener together.

Finishing

Weave in ends, wash and block.

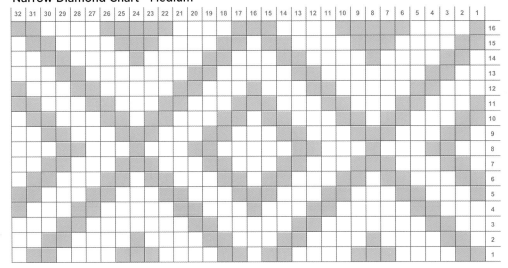

Narrow Diamond Chart - Medium

Legend

☐ knit
knit stitch

☐ MC

▨ CC

Narrow Diamond Foot Chart - Medium

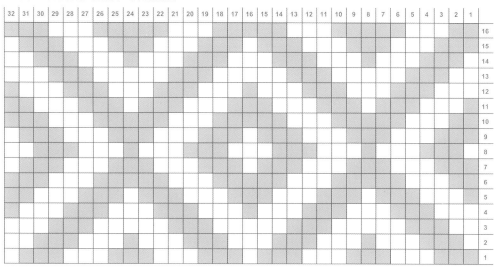

Wide Diamond Chart - Medium

Wide Diamond Foot Chart - Medium

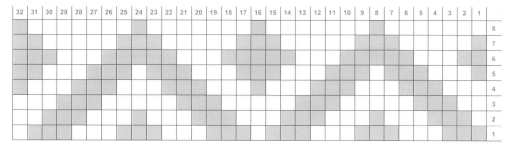

Narrow Diamond Chart - Large

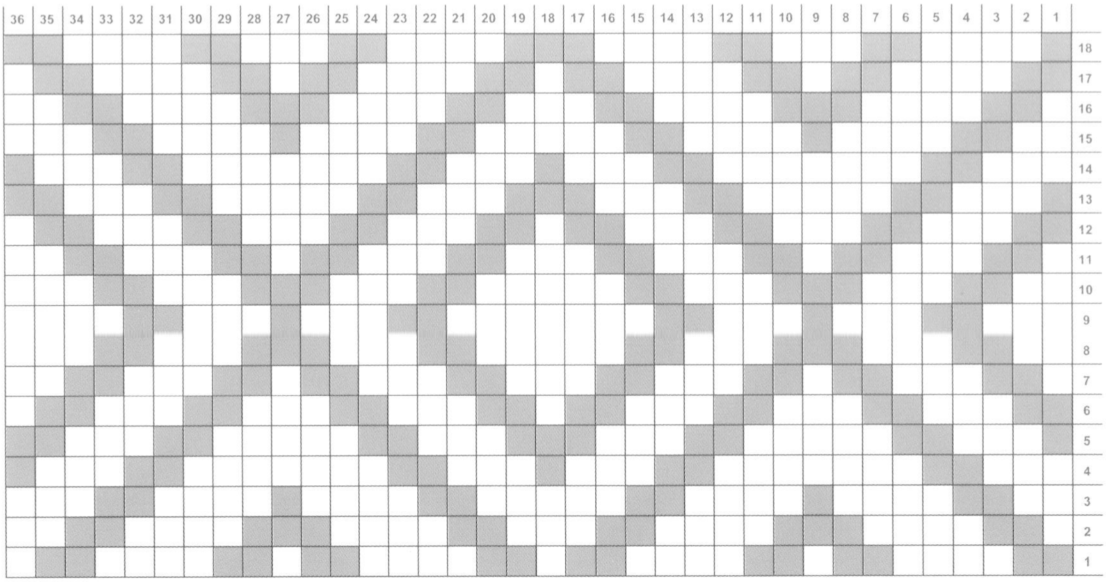
36 35 34 33 32 31 30 29 28 27 26 25 24 23 22 21 20 19 18 17 16 15 14 13 12 11 10 9 8 7 6 5 4 3 2 1
18 17 16 15 14 13 12 11 10 9 8 7 6 5 4 3 2 1

Narrow Diamond Foot Chart - Large

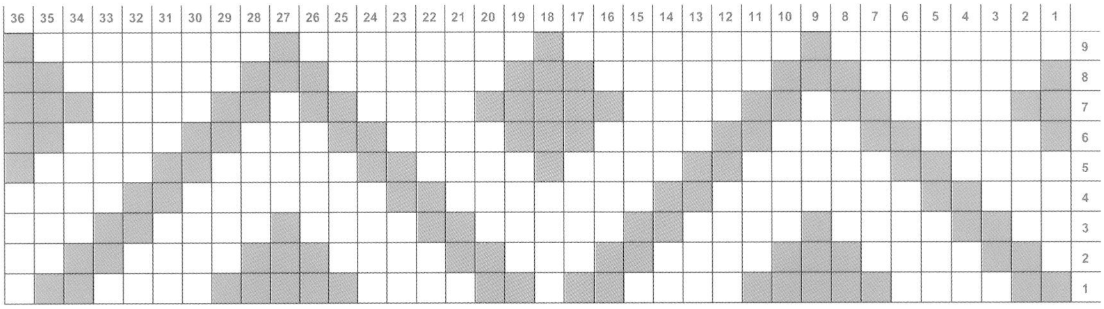
36 35 34 33 32 31 30 29 28 27 26 25 24 23 22 21 20 19 18 17 16 15 14 13 12 11 10 9 8 7 6 5 4 3 2 1
9 8 7 6 5 4 3 2 1

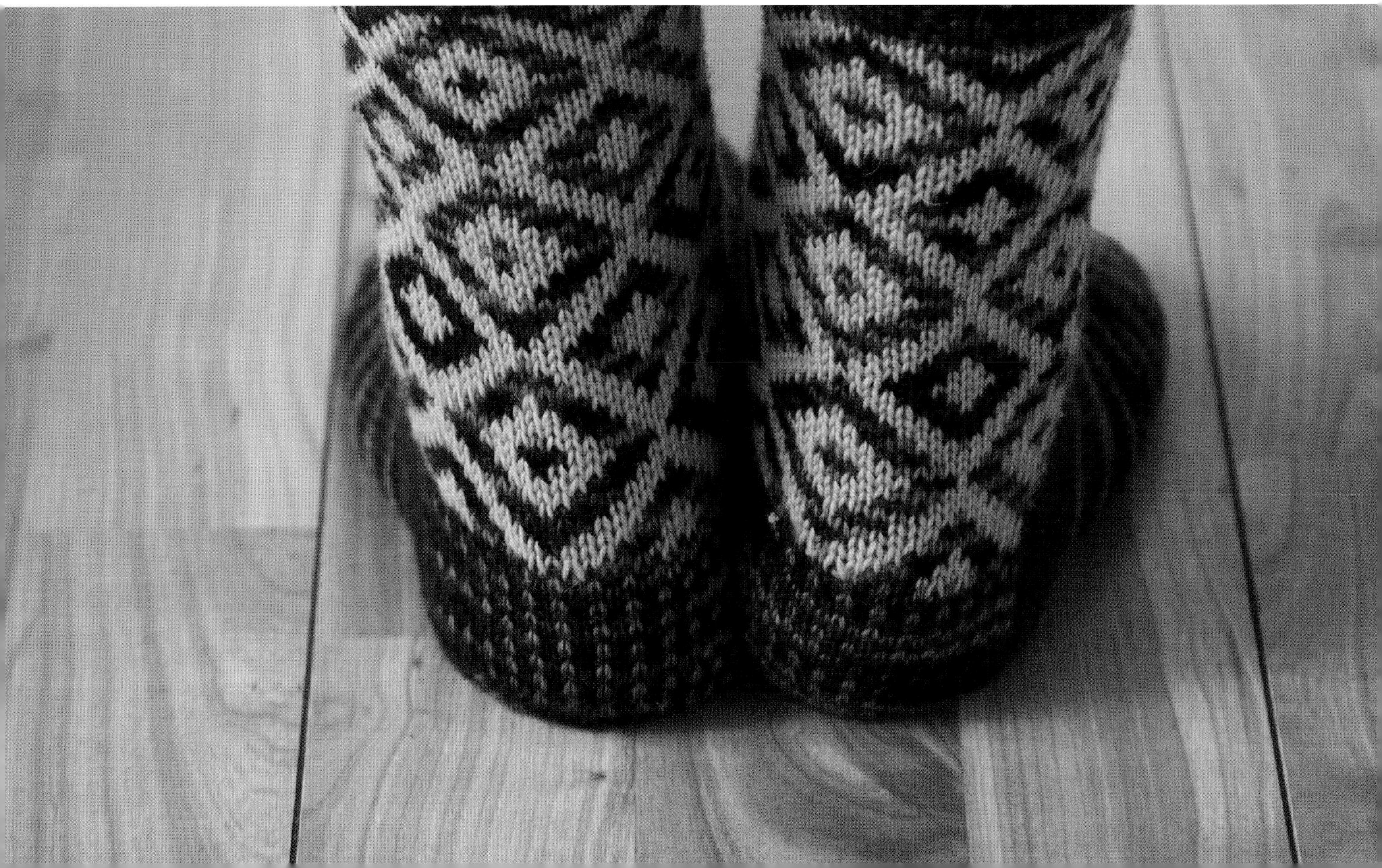

Wide Diamond Chart - Large

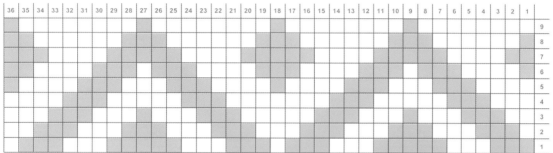

Wide Diamond Foot Chart - Large

TWIRLA SOCKS

by Amanda Schwabe

FINISHED MEASUREMENTS

7.5 (8.5, 9.5)" foot circumference, 7.25 (8, 8.75)" leg circumference x 8.5 (9.75, 11)" foot length, blocked.
Sock should be worn with up to 1" of negative ease.

YARN

Knit Picks Hawthorne Fingering Multi Yarn (80% Superwash Fine Highland Wool, 20% Polyamide (Nylon); 357 yards/100g): MC Goose Hollow 26430, 1 hank.
Knit Picks Hawthorne Fingering Kettle Dye Yarn (80% Superwash Fine Highland Wool, 20% Polyamide (Nylon); 357 yard/100g): C1 Turkish Delight 26691, 1 hank

NEEDLES

US 1 (2.25mm) DPNs or two 24" circular needles for two circulars technique, or one 32" or longer circular needle for Magic Loop technique, or size to obtain gauge

NOTIONS

Yarn Needle
Stitch Markers
Cable Needle (optional)

GAUGE

34 sts and 52 rnds = 4" over Chart A in the rnd, blocked
38 sts and 52 rnds = 4" in Charts B & C in the rnd, blocked.
34 sts and 52 rnds = 4" in St st in the round, blocked

Twirla Socks

Notes:

The Twirla socks use an easy but effective technique: slipped stitch columns! They are so easy to do, and they make such pretty patterns. These socks look like they're made with complex colorwork, but you'll only ever use one color per round.

Twirla also features the Strong Heel method, a roomy, comfortable heel with a gusset that is increased during the leg portion, with no flap or picking up of stitches necessary!

The 2-st cables are so tiny that I like to work them without a cable needle, or with a locking stitch marker as a cable needle, to keep the work from getting unruly.

Slip all sts P-wise unless otherwise indicated, and work all rows of the charts from right to left as RS rows..

Twisted Rib (worked in the round over multiples of 4 sts)
All Rnds: (K2 TBL, P2) to end.

Chart A Cable Panel (in the rnd over 10 sts)
Rnd 1: With C1, K10.
Rnd 2: With MC, Sl1, K8, Sl1.
Rnd 3: With C1, 1/1 LC, K6, 1/1 RC.
Rnd 4: With MC, K1, Sl1, K6, Sl1, K1.
Rnd 5: With C1, K1, 1/1 LC, K4, 1/1 RC, K1.
Rnd 6: With MC, K2, Sl1, K4, Sl1, K2.
Rnd 7: With C1, K2, 1/1 LC, K2, 1/1 RC, K2.
Rnd 8: With MC, K3, Sl1, K2, Sl1, K3.
Rnd 9: With C1, K3, 1/1 LC, 1/1 RC, K3.
Rnd 10: With MC, K4, Sl2, K4.
Rnd 11: With C1, K4, 1/1 RC, K4.
Rnd 12: Repeat Rnd 10.
Rnd 13: With C1, K3, 1/1 RC, 1/1 LC, K3.
Rnd 14: Repeat Rnd 8.
Rnd 15: With C1, K2, 1/1 RC, K2, 1/1 LC, K2.
Rnd 16: Repeat Rnd 6.
Rnd 17: With C1, K1, 1/1 RC, K4, 1/1 LC, K1.
Rnd 18: Repeat Rnd 4.
Rnd 19: With C1, 1/1 RC, K6, 1/1 LC.
Rnd 20: Repeat Rnd 2.
Rep Rnds 1-20 for pattern.

Chart B Cable Panel (in the rnd over 16 (20, 24) sts)
Rnd 1: With C1, [Sl1, K3] 3 (4, 5) times, Sl1, K2, Sl1.
Rnd 2: With MC, K3, [1/1 RC, K2] 2 (3, 4) times, 1/1 RC, K3.
Rnd 3: With C1, Sl1, K2, [Sl1, K3] 3 (4, 5) times, Sl1.
Rnd 4: With MC, [K2, 1/1 RC] 4 (5, 6) times.
Rnd 5: With C1, Sl1, K1, [Sl1, K3] 3 (4, 5) times, Sl2.
Rnd 6: With MC, K1, [1/1 RC, K2] 3 (4, 5) times, 1/1 RC, K1.
Rnd 7: With C1, Sl2, [K3, Sl1] 3 (4, 5) times, K1, Sl1.
Rnd 8: With MC, [1/1 RC, K2] 4 (5, 6) times.
Rep Rnds 1-8 for pattern.

Chart C Cable Panel (in the rnd over 16 (20, 24) sts)
Rnd 1: With C1, Sl1, K2, [Sl1, K3] 3 (4, 5) times, Sl1.
Rnd 2: With MC, K3, [1/1 LC, K2] 2 (3, 4) times, 1/1 LC, K3.
Rnd 3: With C1, [Sl1, K3] 3 (4, 5) times, Sl1, K2, Sl1.

Rnd 4: With MC, [1/1 LC, K2] 4 (5, 6) times.
Rnd 5: With C1, Sl2, [K3, Sl1] 3 (4, 5) times, K1, Sl1.
Rnd 6: With MC, K1, [1/1 LC, K2] 3 (4, 5) times, 1/1 LC, K1.
Rnd 7: With C1, Sl1, K1, [Sl1, K3] 3 (4, 5) times, Sl2.
Rnd 8: With MC, [K2, 1/1 LC] 4 (5, 6) times.
Rep Rnds 1-8 for pattern

1 Over 1 Left Cross (1/1 LC): Sl1 st to CN and hold in front, K1, K1 from CN.
1 Over 1 Right Cross (1/1 RC): Sl1 st to CN and hold in back, K1, K1 from CN.

DIRECTIONS

Cuff
Using MC, CO 64 (72, 80) sts. Join for working in the round, being careful not to twist sts. PM for beginning of rnd. Work in Twisted Rib until cuff measures 1" from CO edge.

Leg
Join C1 but do not cut MC.
From now until Foot, all odd-numbered rounds will be worked in C1, and all even-numbered rounds will be worked in MC.

PM at beginnings and endings of Charts:
Rnd 1: K3, work Chart A, K3, work Chart B, K3, work Chart A, K3, work Chart C.

Continue working in pattern as set, SM as you come to them and repeating Charts from their beginning as required, until Chart A has been worked 3 times.

Heel Increases
Rnd 1: K1, M1L, K2, SM, work Chart A, SM, K2, M1R, K1, SM, work Chart B, SM, K1, M1L, K2, SM, work Chart A, SM, K2, M1R, K1, SM, work Chart C. 4 sts inc. 68 (76, 84) sts.
Rnds 2-4: K to M, SM, work Chart A, SM, K to M, SM, work Chart B, SM, K to M, SM, work Chart A, SM, K to M, SM, work Chart C.
Rnd 5: K1, M1L, K to M, SM, work Chart A, SM, K to 1 st before M, M1R, K1, SM, work Chart B, SM, K1, M1L, K to M, SM, work Chart A, SM, K to 1 st before M, M1R, K1, SM, work Chart C. 4 sts inc.

Repeat Rnds 2-5 6 (7, 8) times more until there are 96 (108, 120) sts.

Work Rnds 2-3 once more.

Work Rnd 4 partially once, ending with 15 (17, 19) sts unworked at end of round.

PM for new beginning of round. Rearrange sts without working them so next 64 (72, 80) sts are on one needle to work back and forth for Heel Turn, and last 32 (36, 40) sts are resting on other needle(s) (these are the Instep sts and will be worked later, after the Heel Turn is complete). At this point, both Chart A panels should be centered on Instep sts and Heel sts.

Heel Turn
Cut C1, leaving a 6" tail for sewing in later, and rejoin to work the heel turn. Do not break MC.
Row 1 (RS): Using C1, K 34 (38, 42), SSK, K1, turn.
Row 2 (WS): Sl1 P-wise WYIF, P5, P2tog, P1, turn.

Row 3: Sl1 P-wise WYIB, K to 1 st before gap, SSK, K1, turn.
Row 4: Sl1 P-wise WYIF, P to 1 st before gap, P2tog, P1, turn.

Rep Rows 3-4 11 (13, 15) more times. 38 (42, 46) heel sts remain, including 3 sts on either side of gaps.

Row 5: Sl1 P-wise WYIB, K to 1 st before gap, SSK, turn.
Row 6: Sl1 P-wise WYIF, P to 1 st before gap, P2tog, turn.

Rep Rows 5-6 once more. 34 (38, 42) heel sts remain, including 1 st on either side of gaps.

Row 7 (RS): Sl1 P-wise WYIB, K30 (34, 38), SSK, do not turn work. 33 (37, 41) Heel sts.

Resume working in the rnd and work Instep sts as follows:
Size 7.5 only: K11, work Chart A, K11. 32 Instep sts.
Size 8.5 only: Sl1, K12, work Chart A, K12, Sl1. 36 Instep sts.
Size 9.5 only: K1, Sl1, K13, work Chart A, K13, Sl1, K1. 40 Instep sts.

Foot

Rnd 1: With MC, K2tog, K31 (35, 39) Sole sts, K11 (13, 15), work Chart A, K11 (13, 15). 64 (72, 80) sts.
Rnd 2: With C1, K 32 (36, 40) Sole sts, work all Instep sts as below for your size:
Size 7.5 only: K11, work Chart A, K11.
Size 8.5 only: Sl1, K12, work Chart A, K12, Sl1.
Size 9.5 only: K1, Sl1, K13, work Chart A, K13, Sl1, K1.
Rnd 3: With MC, K all Sole sts, K11 (13, 15), work Chart A, K11 (13, 15).

Rep Rnds 2-3 until foot measures approximately 6.75 (7.75, 8.75)" OR 1.75 (2, 2.25)" less than desired length.

Toe

Cut C1 and use MC for Toe.

If necessary, divide sts evenly over 2 needles for toe shaping, having the 32 (36, 40) Sole sts on the first needle and the 32 (36, 40) Instep sts on the second needle.

Rnd 1: K1, SSK, K to last 3 Sole sts, K2tog, K1. Repeat for Instep sts.
Rnd 2: K to end of round.

Rep Rnds 1-2 until 20 sts remain, 10 sts on each needle, ending after a Rnd 1.

Close toe by using either of the following two options.
Option 1: Graft remaining sts together using Kitchener St.
Option 2: [K2tog] to end. Cut yarn and thread tail through remaining sts, draw tight to close.

Finishing

Weave in ends. Wash and block.

Chart A

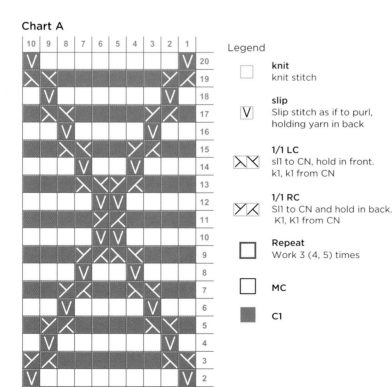

Legend

	knit	knit stitch
V	slip	Slip stitch as if to purl, holding yarn in back
XX	1/1 LC	sl1 to CN, hold in front. k1, k1 from CN
XX	1/1 RC	Sl1 to CN and hold in back. K1, K1 from CN
	Repeat	Work 3 (4, 5) times
	MC	
▓	C1	

Chart B

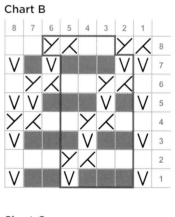

Chart C

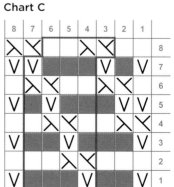

WESTNEY SOCKS

by Dana Gervais

FINISHED MEASUREMENTS

7 (8, 9, 10)" finished circumference, choose a circumference that is 10% less than the wearer's actual foot circumference as measured at the widest part of the foot. Foot length is customizable

YARN

Knit Picks Hawthorne Fingering Multi (80% Superwash Fine Highland Wool, 20% Polyamide (Nylon); 357 yards/100g): Rose City 26432, 1 (2, 2, 2) balls

NEEDLES

US 1 (2.25mm) DPNs, or two 24" circular needles for two circulars technique, or one 32" or longer circular needle for Magic Loop technique, or size to obtain gauge

NOTIONS

Yarn Needle
Stitch Markers
Cable needle

GAUGE

32 sts and 48 rows = 4" in St st in the round, blocked.
32 sts and 48 rows = 4" in Westney st pattern st in the round, blocked

Westney Socks

Notes:

These uniquely textured socks are worked top down starting with the cuff, with the Westney stitch pattern starting at the top of the leg and continuing on the back of the leg and top of the foot. The sole is worked in stockinette. The pattern features a heel flap and gusset and a rounded toe that is grafted closed using Kitchener Stitch. Written instructions are provided for the smallest size with instructions for the other sizes appearing in parentheses; if there are no parentheses, the instruction applies to all sizes.

Westney Stitch Pattern (in the round over a multiple of 8 sts)

Rnd 1: *Work Gathered Stitch, K4; rep from * to end.

Rnds 2-5: K all sts.

Rnd 6: *K4, work Gathered Stitch; rep from * to end.

Rnd 7-10: K all sts.

Gathered Stitch

K the next 4 sts then transfer those sts to a CN being careful not to change the order of the sts, wrap the working yarn loosely around the sts counter clockwise 4 times, return the sts to the RH needle.

DIRECTIONS

Cuff

CO 56 (64, 72, 80) sts, PM to mark beginning of rnd and join for working in the rnd being careful not to twist sts.

Rnd 1: (K2, P2) to end.

Rep Rnd 1 twelve times or until work measures 1" from CO edge.

Leg

Work Rnds 1-10 of the Westney stitch pattern until work measures 6" or desired length from CO edge, ending after any rnd.

Heel Flap

The heel flap is worked back and forth across the last 24 (32, 32, 40) sts.

Set Up: Work the Westney stitch pattern across the first 32 (32, 40, 40) sts then work Row 1. Note the last pattern rnd worked.
Row 1(RS): *Sl1, K1; rep from * to end.
Row 2 (WS): Sl1, P to end.

Repeat these 2 rows 16 (16, 20, 20) times total, ending after a WS row.

Turning The Heel

Row 1 (RS): Sl1, K11 (15, 15, 19), SSK, K1, turn work.
Row 2 (WS): Sl1, P1, P2tog, P1, turn work.
Row 3: Sl1, K2, SSK, K1, turn work.
Row 4: Sl1, P3, P2tog, P1, turn work.
Row 5: Sl1, K4, SSK, K1, turn work.
Row 6: Sl1, P5, P2tog, P1, turn work.

Cont as established, working one more st on each row before the dec until all sts have been worked, ending the last row(s) with SSK/P2tog if necessary. 12 (16, 16, 20) heel sts remain.

Shaping The Gussets

K across heel sts, PU and K 16 (16, 20, 20) sts along edge of heel flap, SM (beg of rnd), cont Westney st pattern as established across instep sts, PM to separate instep sts from sole sts, PU and K 16 (16, 20, 20) sts along edge of heel flap, K to end of rnd. 76 (80, 96, 100) total sts.

Rnd 1: Cont Westney stitch pattern as established to M, SM, K1, SSK, K to last 3 sts, K2tog, K1. 2 sts dec.
Rnd 2: K all sts.

Repeat Rnds 1-2 10 (8, 12, 10) times until 24 (32, 32, 40) sole sts remain.

Foot

Cont working Westney stitch pattern as established across instep sts while working sole sts in St st until foot length measures 1.5 (1.75, 1.75, 2)" less than desired finished length.

Shaping The Toe

Sizes 7" and 9" Only

Set Up Rnd: K one rnd transferring the first 2 and the last 2 instep sts to the sole. Move M to divide instep and sole sts evenly. 28 (36) instep sts and 28 (36) sole sts.

All Sizes:
Rnd 1: K1, SSK, K to 3 sts before M, K2tog, K1, SM, K1, SSK, K to last 3 sts, K2tog, K1. 4 sts dec.
Rnd 2: K all sts.

Repeat Rnds 1-2 7 (8, 9, 10) times until 28 (32, 36, 40) sts remain.

Repeat Rnd 1 only 3 (4, 4, 5) times until 16 (16, 20, 20) sts remain.

Finishing

Arrange all instep sts on a single needle and all sole sts on a single needle. Use Kitchener Stitch to graft instep and sole sts together. Weave in ends and block.

Westney Chart

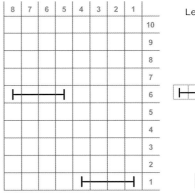

Legend

Gathered Stitch
K the next 4 sts then transfer sts to a CN. Being careful not to change the order of the sts, wrap the working yarn loosely around the sts counter clockwise 4 times, return the sts to the RH needle

knit
knit stitch

OSCILLATORY SOCKS

by Abbey Morris

FINISHED MEASUREMENTS

7.75 (8.75, 10)" leg circumference x 7.25 (7.25, 7.5)" leg length before heel

YARN

Knit Picks Hawthorne Fingering Multi Yarn (80% Superwash Fine Highland Wool, 20% Polyamide (Nylon); 357 yards/100g): Abernathy 26863, 1 hank

NEEDLES

US 1 (2.25mm) DPNs, or two 24" circular needles for two circulars technique, or one 32" or longer circular needle for Magic Loop technique, or size to obtain gauge

NOTIONS

Yarn Needle
Stitch Markers
Cable Needle

GAUGE

29 sts and 40 rows = 4" in Zig Zag Stitch Pattern in the round, blocked.
29 sts and 40 rows = 4" in Stockinette Stitch in the round, blocked

Oscillatory Socks

Notes:

These stylish socks are worked from the top-down with a square heel. After working a K1, P1 rib, the main Zig Zag Stitch Pattern is worked around the leg, down across the top of the foot and the wedge toe is closed using Kitchener Stitch.

Left Twist (LT)
Sl1 to CN, hold in front, K1, K1 from CN

Right Twist (RT)
Skip first st, K into 2nd st, then K skipped st. Sl both sts from needle together OR K2tog leaving sts on LH needle, then K first st again, Sl both sts off needle.

K1, P1 Rib (in the round over even number of sts)
Rnd 1: *K1, P1, repeat from * to end.

Repeat Rnd 1 for pattern

Zig Zag Stitch Pattern (in the round over multiples of 8 sts)
Rnds 1 & 2: *K7, Sl1 P-wise, rep from * to end.

Rnd 3: *K6, RT, rep from * to end.

Rnds 4 & 5: *K5, Sl1 P-wise, K2, rep from * to end.

Rnd 6: *K4, RT, K2, rep from * to end.

Rnds 7 & 8: *K3, Sl1 P-wise, K4, rep from * to end.

Rnd 9: *K2, RT, K4, rep from * to end.

Rnds 10 & 11: *K1, Sl1 P-wise, K6, rep from * to end.

Rnd 12: *RT, K6, rep from * to end.

Rnds 13 & 14: *Sl1 P-wise, K7, rep from * to end.

Rnd 15: *LT, K6, rep from * to end.

Rnds 16 & 17: *K2, Sl1 P-wise, K5, rep from * to end.

Rnd 18: *K2, LT, K4, rep from * to end.

Rnds 19 & 20: *K4, Sl1 P-wise, K3, rep from * to end.

Rnd 21: *K4, LT, K2, rep from * to end.

Rnds 22 & 23: *K6, Sl1 P-wise, K1, rep from * to end.

Rnd 24: *K6, LT, rep from * to end.

Repeat Rnds 1-24 for pattern

If working from chart, follow all chart rows from left to right, reading them as RS rows.

DIRECTIONS

Cuff
Using Long Tail Method, CO 56 (64, 72) sts. Divide sts evenly over needles. PM and join in the rnd, being careful not to twist the sts.

Ribbing
Work in K1, P1 Rib for 12 (12, 14) rnds.

Leg
Work Rnds 1-24 of the Zig Zag Stitch Pattern from either the written instructions or chart twice then repeat Rnds 1-12 of the Zig Zag Stitch Pattern once.

Heel Flap
The heel flap is worked back and forth over the first 28 (32, 36) sts of the rnd. Rearrange stitches as needed.

Row 1 (RS): *Sl1, K1; repeat from * to end.

Row 2 (WS): Sl1 P-wise, P to end.

Repeat Rows 1-2 ten (eleven, twelve) more times until 22 (24, 26) rows have been worked.

Heel Turn
Row 1 (RS): Sl1, K15 (18, 20), SSK, K1, turn. 27 (31, 35) sts.

Row 2 (WS): Sl1 P-wise, P6 (8, 9), P2tog, P1, turn. 26 (30, 34) sts.

Row 3: Sl1, K7 (9, 10), SSK, K1, turn. 25 (29, 33) sts.

Row 4: Sl1 P-wise, P8 (10, 11), P2tog, P1, turn. 24 (28, 32) sts.

Row 5: Sl1, K9 (11, 12), SSK, K1, turn. 23 (27, 31) sts.

Row 6: Sl1 P-wise, P10 (12, 13), P2tog, P1, turn. 22 (26, 30) sts.

Row 7: Sl1, K11 (13, 14), SSK, K1, turn. 21 (25, 29) sts.

Row 8: Sl1 P-wise, P12 (14, 15), P2tog, P1, turn. 20 (24, 28) sts.

Row 9: Sl1, K13 (15, 16), SSK, K1, turn. 19 (23, 27) sts.

Row 10: Sl1 P-wise, P14 (16, 17), P2tog, P1, turn. 18 (22, 26) sts.

7.75" Size Only:

Row 11: Sl1, K15, SSK, turn. 17 (-, -) sts.

Row 12: Sl1 P-wise, P14, P2tog, turn. 16 (-, -) sts.

8.75" Size Only:

Row 11: Sl1, K17, SSK, K1, turn. – (21, -) sts.

Row 12: Sl1 P-wise, P18, P2tog, turn. – (20, -) sts.

10" Size Only:

Row 11: Sl1, K18, SSK, K1, turn. – (-, 25) sts.

Row 12: Sl1 P-wise, P19, P2tog, P1, turn. – (-, 24) sts.

Row 13: Sl1, K20, SSK, turn. – (-, 23) sts.

Row 14: Sl1 P-wise, P20, P2tog, turn. – (-, 22) sts.

Set Up Rnd (All Sizes): K across heel, PU and K 16 (17, 19) sts down heel flap, PM, K4 (0, 4) sts, cont working in Zig Zag Stitch Pattern from either chart or written instructions across next 24 (32, 32) sts starting with Rnd 13 across instep, PM, PU and K 16 (17, 19) sts up the heel flap. 76 (86, 96) sts.

K 8 (10, 11) sts to the middle of heel and PM. The beginning of the rnd now starts in the middle of the heel.

Gusset
Rnd 1: K to last 3sts before M, K2tog, K1, SM, K4 (0, 4), cont working in Zig Zag Stitch Pattern from either chart or written instructions across next 24 (32, 32) sts, SM, K1, SSK, K to end. 2 sts dec.

Rnd 2: K to M, SM, K4 (0, 4), cont working in Zig Zag Stitch Pattern from chart or written instructions across next 24 (32, 32) sts, SM, K to end.

Repeat Rnds 1-2 ten (eleven, twelve) times until 56 (64, 72) sts remain.

Foot
Rnd 1: K to M, SM, K4 (0, 4), cont working in Zig Zag Stitch Pattern from chart or written instructions across next 24 (32, 32) sts, SM K to end.

Repeat Rnd 1 until foot is 1.5 (1.5, 1.75)" less than desired finished length, ending with an even rnd of the Zig Zag Stitch Pattern.

Toe
Rnd 1 (dec rnd): K to last 3 sts before M, K2tog, K1, SM, K1, SSK, K to last 3 sts before M, K2tog, K1, SM K1, SSK, K to end. 4 sts dec.

Rnd 2: K.

Rep Rnds 1-2 five (five, six) more times until 32 (40, 44) sts remain.

Then rep Rnd 1, three (four, four) more times until 20 (24, 28) sts remain.

K to the first M, and if necessary rearrange the sts so they are even on two needles. Graft ends together using Kitchener Stitch to close the toe.

Finishing
Weave in ends. Wash and block.

Zig Zag Chart

8	7	6	5	4	3	2	1	
⋏	⋏							24
	V							23
	V							22
		⋏	⋏					21
			V					20
			V					19
				⋏	⋏			18
					V			17
					V			16
						⋏	⋏	15
							V	14
							V	13
						⋏	⋏	12
							V	11
							V	10
				⋏	⋏			9
					V			8
					V			7
		⋏	⋏					6
			V					5
			V					4
⋏	⋏							3
	V							2
	V							1

Legend

□ **knit**
knit stitch

V **slip**
Slip stitch as if to purl, holding yarn in back

⋏ **Right Twist**
Skip first st, K into 2nd st, then K skipped st. Sl both sts from needle together OR K2tog leaving sts on LH needle, then K first st again, Sl both sts off needle

⋏ **Left Twist**
sl1 to CN, hold in front. k1, k1 from CN

HEAVENLY SHADES SOCKS

by Katherine Rollins

FINISHED MEASUREMENTS

7 (8, 9)" foot circumference

YARN

Knit Picks Hawthorne Fingering Multi Yarn (80% Superwash Fine Highland Wool, 20% Polyamide (Nylon); 357 yards/100g): MC Alberta Arts 26446, 1 hank.

Knit Picks Hawthorne Fingering Kettle Dye Yarn (80% Superwash Fine Highland Wool, 20% Polyamide (Nylon); 357 yards/100g): C2 Poseidon 26693, 1 hank.

NEEDLES

US 2 (3mm) DPN's, or two 24" circular needles for two circulars technique, or one 32" or longer circular needle for Magic Loop technique, or size to obtain gauge.

US 3 (3.25mm) DPNs, or two 24" circular needles for two circulars technique, or one 32" or longer circular needle for Magic Loop technique, or one size larger than needle used to obtain gauge (optional).

NOTIONS

Yarn Needle
Stitch Marker

GAUGE

32 sts and 42 rows = 4" in stranded St st in the round, blocked.

Heavenly Shades Socks

Notes:

"Heavenly shades of night are falling, it's twilight time." - The Platters, *Twilight Time*.

These socks are knit toe-up and have a short row heel. They begin with a closed-toe cast on of your choice such as Judy's Magic Cast On, and end with a stretchy bind off. Knitting a swatch is strongly recommended to ensure stitch gauge for fit. The stranded pattern makes a firm fabric with a snug fit. You may wish to switch to a size larger needle to knit the leg section.

W&T

Pull the working yarn between the needles to the opposite side, slip the next st, pull the working yarn back between the needles to wrap around that st, slip the st back to the left needle. Turn the work.

For a video demonstration of how to work a Wrap & Turn, see http://tutorials.knitpicks.com/wptutorials/short-rows-wrap-and-turn-or-wt/

Judy's Magic Cast On

For a video demonstration of how to work Judy's Magic Cast On, see
http://tutorials.knitpicks.com/wptutorials/judys-magic-cast-on/

Stretchy Bind Off

For a video demonstration of how to work a stretchy bind off, see http://tutorials.knitpicks.com/wptutorials/go-your-own-way-socks-toe-up-part-7-binding-off/

DIRECTIONS

Toe

With MC, using a closed-toe cast-on (see Notes), CO 28 (32, 36) sts.
K 1 rnd.

Work increase rnds as follows:
Inc Rnd 1: *K1, M1L, K12 (14, 16), M1R, K1; rep from * once more.
Inc Rnd 2: K.

Repeat Rnds 1-2 until there are 56 (64, 72) total sts.

Foot

Attach C1 and begin working appropriate Shades Chart 1 for selected size Small, Medium or Large. Work each row of the chart twice for each round. Work all rows of the Shades Chart 1 once.

Work each row of the Shades Chart 2, repeating 14 (16, 18) times to complete a rnd. Repeat Shades Chart 2 in pattern as established until the foot length is 2" less than the desired total foot length. Work 28 (32, 36) sts and note the last row of Shades Chart 2 worked before beginning to shape the heel on the remaining sts

Heel

Using C1 (or MC if desired), work the heel across the last 28 (32, 36) sts of the round only.

Row 1: K to 1 st before the last st, W&T the last st.
Row 2: P to 1 st before the last st, W&T the last st.
Row 3: K to 1 st before the wrapped st, W&T.
Row 4: P to 1 st before the wrapped st, W&T.

Repeat Rows 3 & 4 until 7 (8, 9) sts are wrapped on each side with 14 (16, 18) unwrapped sts in the center. This completes the first half of the heel.

Row 1: K across the center sts to the first wrapped st. K the st and the wrap together. W&T the next st (now this st has two wraps).
Row 2: P to the first wrapped st. P the st and the wrap together. W&T the next st (now this st has two wraps).

Repeat the last two rows, knitting or purling the two wraps with the st until all wrapped sts have been worked.

Leg

Begin working in the round again. Continue the Shades Chart 2 by working the row last worked before beginning the heel for 7 (8, 9) times to complete the rnd, then work each chart row as before for 14 (16, 18) times to complete a rnd. Repeat Shades Chart 2 until leg is 3.5" less than desired height, ending on Row 12 of Chart 2.

Begin working appropriate Shades Chart 3 for selected size Small, Medium or Large. Work each row of the chart twice for each round. Work all rows of Shades Chart 3 once. Break C1.

Cuff

With MC
Rnds 1-9: [K2, P2] repeat across the rnd.
Inc Rnd: [K1, KFB, P2] repeat across the rnd
Rnd 11-14: [K2, P3] repeat across the rnd.
BO all sts.

Repeat directions to make second sock.

Finishing

Weave in all ends and block.

Chart 1 Large

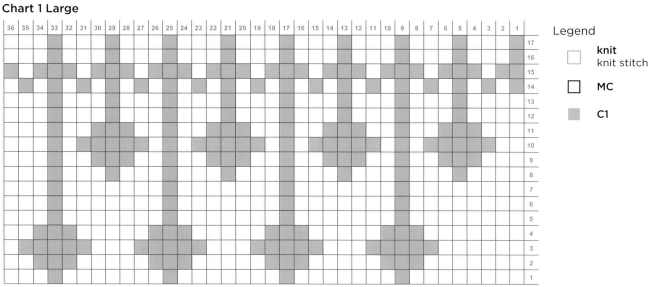

Legend

knit
knit stitch

MC

C1

Chart 1 Medium

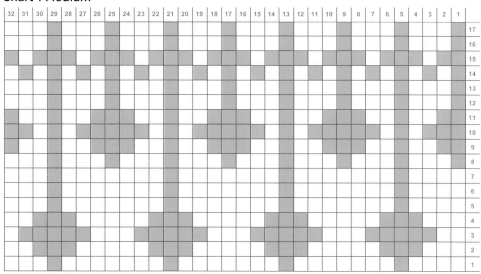

Chart 1 Small

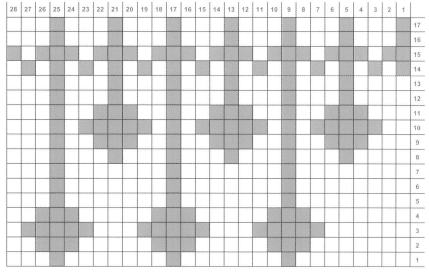

Chart 2 (all sizes) ## Chart 3 Large

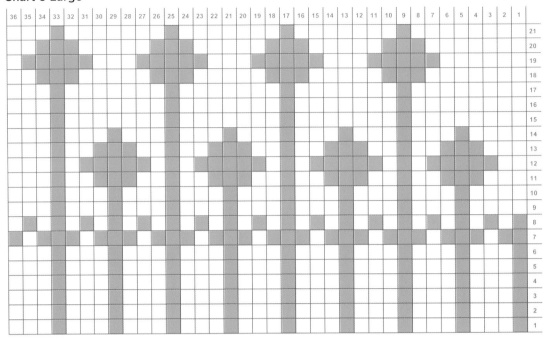

Chart 3 Medium

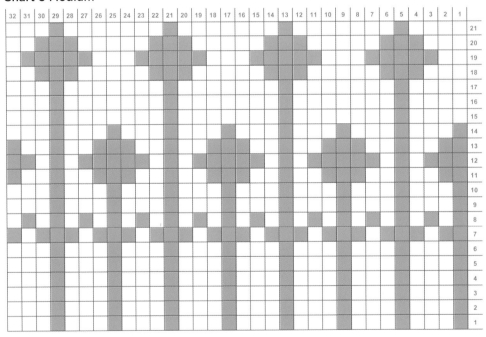

Chart 3 Small

28	27	26	25	24	23	22	21	20	19	18	17	16	15	14	13	12	11	10	9	8	7	6	5	4	3	2	1	
																												21
																												20
																												19
																												18
																												17
																												16
																												15
																												14
																												13
																												12
																												11
																												10
																												9
																												8
																												7
																												6
																												5
																												4
																												3
																												2
																												1

SPARKLE SOCKS

by Violet LeBeaux

FINISHED MEASUREMENTS

7.5" circumference x 8" foot length x 7.5" leg height

If back of leg is worked in plain St st calf circumference is 8". If Picot Edging is worked, leg height is 7.75"

YARN

Knit Picks Stroll Hand Painted Sock Yarn (75% Superwash Merino Wool, 25% Nylon; 462 yards/100g): Make Believe 24770, 1 hank.

NEEDLES

US 3 (3.25mm) two 24" circular needles for two circulars technique, or one 32" or longer circular needle for Magic Loop technique, or size to obtain gauge.

NOTIONS

Yarn Needle
Stitch Markers
Sewing Pins (optional)

GAUGE

24 sts and 44 rnds = 4" in St st, in the round, blocked.
28 sts and 40 rnds = 4" in Sparkle St Pattern, in the round, blocked.

Sparkle Socks

Notes:

Sparkle is a simple sock pattern featuring the slipped Sparkle stitch. The pattern is worked toe up with a stockinette sole and a Fleegle heel. The top is ribbed and has an optional picot edging for a feminine finish. The stitch pattern distributes colors in a textured way that works well with tonal, hand painted and speckle yarns. As the slipped stitch pattern has a bit less elasticity than stockinette there is a stockinette stripe up both sides of the leg area or the option to continue the stockinette of the sole all the way up the back of the leg depending on fit preference.

Note that these stitch patterns require blocking to bring out the star pattern and manipulate the slipped stitches to match the row height of other sections. Before blocking it will not match the height of the stockinette sections and so your knitting will look curved until blocked.

Sparkle St Pattern (in the round over multiples of 4 sts)
Rnds 1-2: *K1, SL3 WYIF; rep from * to end.
Rnd 3: *K2, SL2K, K1; rep from * to end.
Rnds 4-5: K2, *K1, SL3 WYIF; rep from * to last 2 sts, K2.
Rnd 6: K2 *K2, SL2K, K1; rep from * to last 2 sts, K2
Rep Rnds 1-6 for the pattern.

When working charts in the rnd, follow all chart rows from right to left, reading them as RS rows.

Magic Loop (optional)
A technique using one large circular needle to knit small circumferences. A great tutorial can be found here: http://tutorials.knitpicks.com/wptutorials/magic-loop/

Judy's Magic Cast On
Step by step instructions for Judy's Magic Cast on can be found here: http://tutorials.knitpicks.com/wptutorials/judys-magic-cast-on/

Lifted Increases
Left Lifted Increase (LLI): K 1 into the st below the previously worked st on the right needle.
Right Lifted Increase (RLI): K 1 into the st below the next st on left needle.

SL2K
Insert right needle under the two horizontal strands of yarn in front of the previous rnds. K next st off left needle. Slide the 2 two strands over the new st and off the needles.

Fleegle Heel
A heel technique using lifted increases for the gusset and short rows for the decreases.

Picot Edging (optional)
This edging is knit flat then folded in half and joined by knitting a round in which every stitch on the left needle is K2tog with a stitch picked up from an earlier round in the knitting. The piece is then bound off.

If you have trouble keeping the folded edge in place while knitting, use sewing pins to hold in place. If you are not comfortable knitting together stitch by stitch you can opt to knit the join row regularly and then sew the edge down while finishing.

DIRECTIONS

Foot

Toe
CO 16 sts over 2 needles using Judy's Magic Cast On and PM to indicate the beginning of the rnd.
Rnd 1: K to end.
Rnd 2: Needle 1: *K1, RLI, K to last st, LLI, K1. Needle 2: Rep from * to end. 4 sts inc.

Rep Rnds 1-2 another 7 times. 48 sts, 24 sts on each Needle.

If you require a larger size, continue repeating Rnds 1-2, until the desired width (comfortable fit around your first 4 toes) and number of stitches on one needle matches stitch count for Sparkle St Pattern (multiples of 4 sts).

Foot
This section has the Sparkle St Pattern on the instep (Needle 1) and a St st sole (Needle 2) to maintain a stretchy fit.

Rnds 1-6: Needle 1: Work Sparkle St Pattern beginning with Rnd 1. Needle 2: K to end.
Rep Rnds 1-6 until the piece measures 4.5" from start of the pattern section ending on Rnd 6.

If you require a longer foot size, continue working in established pattern until the sock reaches the ankle bend when worn and ending on Rnd 6.

Heel
The heel is knit using the Fleegle Heel Technique which creates a heel gusset with increases, and then is turned with short rows.

Gusset
Rnd 1: Needle 1: Work Sparkle St Pattern. Needle 2: K to end.
Rnd 2: Needle 1: Work Sparkle St Pattern. Needle 2: K2, RLI, K to last 2sts, LLI, K2. 2 sts inc.

Rep Rnds 1-2 10 more times (Needle 1: 24 sts, Needle 2: 46 sts) OR if knitting a larger size, repeat until you have 2 less than double the original number of sts on Needle 2. (e.g. If you started with 30 sts on the second needle, continue increasing until you have 58sts.)

Set Up Rnd: Needle 1: Work Sparkle St Pattern. Needle 2: Move on to Heel Turn Short Rows below. Make note of which Sparkle St Pattern rnd you have just worked.

Heel Turn Short Rows
This section is worked back and forth using only the sts on Needle 2.

PM after half of the sts on Needle 2.

Row 1 (RS): K to 2 sts past M, K2tog, K1, W&T.
Row 2 (WS): Sl1, P to 2 beyond the M, SSP, P1, W&T.
Row 3: Sl1, K to 1 st before gap, K2tog, K1, W&T.
Row 4: Sl1, P to 1 st before gap, SSP, P1, W&T.

Rep Rows 3-4 another 7 times (Needle 1 - 24sts, Needle 2 - 28sts) OR if knitting a larger size rep until the sole has 4 sts more than were originally on the second needle. (e.g. If you started with 30sts and increased to 58sts, continue decreasing until you have 34sts ending on a WS row.)

Next RS Row: K to end of Needle 2.

Leg

This section is worked over both needles in the round. As the Sparkle Stitch Pattern has a little less give due to the slipped stitches, there are two options to continue the leg section: Patterned Leg and Plain Leg.

Patterned Leg Option

This option features the Sparkle St on both front and back with a 4 st stockinette stripe up each side to provide enough stretch for a comfortable fit. If you are making socks for a larger heel you can knit the stockinette section on each end of Needle 2 wider before beginning Sparkle St in the middle. To work out how much stretch you might need, compare your blocked gauge swatch stretched vs. the circumference around the foot at the largest point of the heel.

Rnd 1: Needle 1: Work Sparkle St Pattern Rnd 1. Needle 2: K to end.

Rnd 2-4: Needle 1: continue Sparkle St pattern. Needle 2: K3, continue Sparkle St pattern (at same rnd as Needle 1) until 5 sts before end, K to end.

Rnds 5-7: Needle 1: continue Sparkle St pattern. Needle 2: K3, continue Sparkle St pattern (at same rnd as Needle 1) until 1 st before end, K to end.

Repeat Rnds 2-7 until the piece measures 4.5" if working ribbing only, or 4.25" if working ribbing and Picot Edging, from end of the heel on Needle 2 OR if knitting a larger size, repeat Rnd 2 until work reaches the desired length minus 1" for the ribbing or 1.25" if working the optional Picot Edging.

Move on to the Ribbing section.

Plain Leg Option

This option features the stitch pattern on front only with stockinette on the back to match the sole and heel. This version has a stretchier width and is therefore suggested for a wider range of ankle and leg fits.

Rnd 1: Needle 1: Work Sparkle St Pattern. Needle 2: K to end. Repeat Rnd 1 until the piece measures 4.5" if working ribbing only, or 4.25" if working ribbing and Picot Edging, from end of the heel on Needle 2 OR if knitting a larger size, repeat Rnd 1 until work reaches the desired length minus 1" for the ribbing or 1.25" if working the optional Picot Edging.

Move on to the Ribbing section.

Ribbing

Rnds 1-10: *K1, P1; rep from * to end.

If adding the optional Picot Edging, continue on to that section, otherwise BO all sts using a stretchy BO.

Optional Picot Edging

Rnd 1-2: *K1, P1; rep from * to end.
Rnd 3: *YO, K2tog; rep from * to end.
Rnd 4-5: *P1, K1; rep from * to end.
Fold the edge of the knitting back on itself so that Rnd 3 forms the picot edging.
Rnd 6 (Join Rnd): K each st from your needle together with the matching one behind it from Rnd 1.
BO all sts.

Finishing

If required, sew down edges of Picot Edging. Weave in ends, wash and block to diagram.

Full Back Stitch Chart - Needle 2

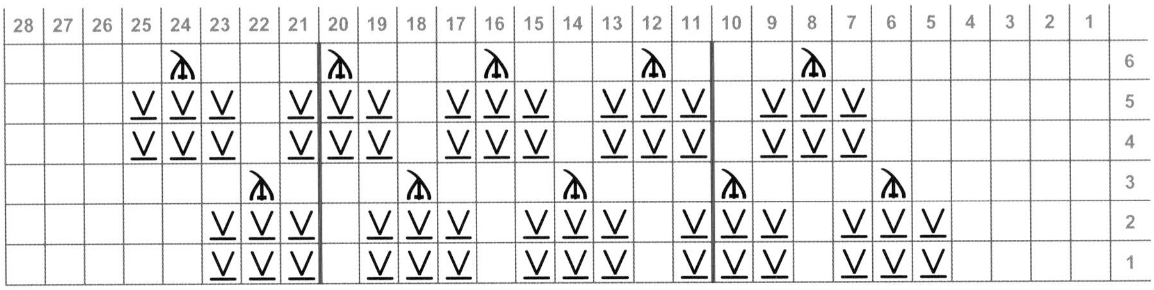

28	27	26	25	24	23	22	21	20	19	18	17	16	15	14	13	12	11	10	9	8	7	6	5	4	3	2	1	
				▲				▲				▲				▲				▲								6
			V	V	V			V	V	V		V	V	V	V	V	V		V	V	V							5
			V	V	V			V	V	V		V	V	V	V	V	V		V	V	V							4
					▲				▲				▲				▲				▲							3
				V	V	V		V	V	V		V	V	V	V	V	V	V		V	V	V						2
				V	V	V		V	V	V		V	V	V	V	V	V	V		V	V	V						1

Full Instep Stitch Chart - Needle 1

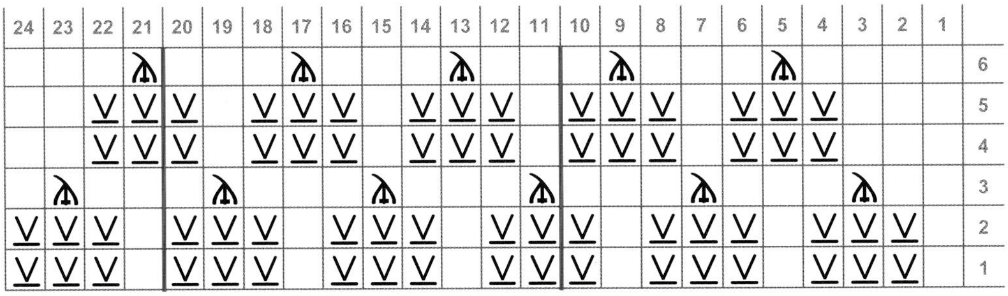

24	23	22	21	20	19	18	17	16	15	14	13	12	11	10	9	8	7	6	5	4	3	2	1	
			▲				▲				▲				▲				▲					6
		V	V	V		V	V	V		V	V	V		V	V	V		V	V	V				5
		V	V	V		V	V	V		V	V	V		V	V	V		V	V	V				4
	▲				▲				▲				▲				▲				▲			3
V	V	V		V	V	V		V	V	V		V	V	V		V	V	V		V	V	V		2
V	V	V		V	V	V		V	V	V		V	V	V		V	V	V		V	V	V		1

Legend

knit
knit stitch

slip wyif
V — Slip stitch as if to purl, with yarn in front

Slip 2 Knit
▲ — Insert right needle under the two horizontal strands in front of previous rows. Knit next stitch off left needle. Slide the 2 strands over the new stitch and off the needles

—— **pattern repeat**

Abbreviations

BO	bind off	M	marker		stitch	TBL	through back loop
cn	cable needle	M1	make one stitch	RH	right hand	TFL	through front loop
CC	contrast color	M1L	make one left-leaning	rnd(s)	round(s)	tog	together
CDD	Centered double dec		stitch	RS	right side	W&T	wrap & turn (see
CO	cast on	M1R	make one right-lean-	Sk	skip		specific instructions
cont	continue		ing stitch	Sk2p	sl 1, k2tog, pass		in pattern)
dec	decrease(es)	MC	main color		slipped stitch over	WE	work even
DPN(s)	double pointed	P	purl		k2tog: 2 sts dec	WS	wrong side
	needle(s)	P2tog	purl 2 sts together	SKP	sl, k, psso: 1 st dec	WYIB	with yarn in back
EOR	every other row	PM	place marker	SL	slip	WYIF	with yarn in front
inc	increase	PFB	purl into the front and	SM	slip marker	YO	yarn over
K	knit		back of stitch	SSK	sl, sl, k these 2 sts tog		
K2tog	knit two sts together	PSSO	pass slipped stitch	SSP	sl, sl, p these 2 sts tog		
KFB	knit into the front and		over		tbl		
	back of stitch	PU	pick up	SSSK	sl, sl, sl, k these 3 sts		
K-wise	knitwise	P-wise	purlwise		tog		
LH	left hand	rep	repeat	St st	stockinette stitch		
		Rev St st	reverse stockinette	sts	stitch(es)		

Knit Picks yarn is both luxe and affordable—a seeming contradiction trounced! But it's not just about the pretty colors; we also care deeply about fiber quality and fair labor practices, leaving you with a gorgeously reliable product you'll turn to time and time again.

THIS COLLECTION FEATURES

Stroll
Fingering Weight
75% Superwash Merino Wool,
25% Nylon

Hawthorne Fingering
Fingering Weight
80% Superwash Fine Highland Wool,
25% Polyamide (Nylon)

View these beautiful yarns and
more at www.KnitPicks.com